T0106282

UFO: Angels and the Mayan Calendar

Gerardo Santos

Order this book online at www.trafford.com
or email orders@trafford.com

Most Trafford titles are also available at major online book retailers.

Printed in the United States of America.

ISBN: 978-1-4269-9363-3 (sc)
ISBN: 978-1-4269-9364-0 (hc)
ISBN: 978-1-4269-9365-7 (e)

Library of Congress Control Number: 2011916234

Trafford rev. 12/28/2011

www.trafford.com

North America & international
toll-free: 1 888 232 4444 (USA & Canada)
phone: 250 383 6864 • fax: 812 355 4082

This book is dedicated

To my three oldest children, Evelyn, Gerry, Erika– may you find comfort in the light
To Reyna, for your courage has inspired me
To Sam, thank you for believing in me
To the memory of Dave, you believed in the light
To the memory of Ruben, you came upon the light
To the memory of mom, you introduced me to the light
To my two youngest children, Elisha and Sammy, your sacrifice will not go unrewarded
To the Fifth Generation – you are destined to change the world

INTRODUCTION

Suppose that in the ancient past the UFO was called an IFO – Identified Flying Object, and the IFO, to the ancient scribe, adhered to many names: Falcon, Eagle, Chariot, Cloud, Whirlwind, Heaven, and Spirit are just a few. The UFO is a craft which enters into earth's fifth dimension then enters into dimension thirteenth. Inside the UFO are beings composed of pure thought, they came to earth to fulfill God's plan.

The beings came in response to the start of the new age. They came to assist mankind through the approaching shift in human consciousness. They are the visitors that come to man from the true God, and they came to earth inside their brightly lighted UFOs, and their legacy and their place in human history remains to this very day.

Because the UFO and the IFO are identical, they came to be called the spirit, and since the spirit shares the same message, the being inside the UFO came to be called the messenger. And because the angel is God's messenger, the spirit inside the UFO belongs to the biblical angel; therefore, if logic is to prevail in this perusal – the spirit inside the UFO is one of God's angels!

Now that we perceive that *E.T.* and the angel is one and the same phenomenon -- our concept of the biblical angel will change forever. But doesn't man perceive the UFO phenomenon wrong from the start? The spirit inside the UFO is not the grotesque alien invader who came to earth with a plan to seek and to destroy human society after all! This is absolutely false! The spirit inside the UFO is the biblical angel. This is absolutely true! The Angel has been coming to earth, for thousands of years, as a part of God's plan to liberate the human spirit.

But what went wrong to cause God to require messengers -- the biblical angels -- to enlighten man from his misled deeds within his temporary realm of consciousness? Well, the bible provides the answer with the story of the fall of the angels which sent repercussions down to earth and created the condition man refers to as good and evil. This condition de-generated the human mind to the level man finds it in today. Fortunately for him, the messenger remains faithful and comes to earth to prepare a new generation, for a new awareness, for the new transformation in human consciousness, for the new Age of Aquarius.

Thus, the root of evil originated from the fall of the angels, and the conflict between the messengers from the valley of light and those who fall into the pit of darkness has been an on-going dilemma that shall climax by the end of the Age of Aquarius. An Agenda, from the fallen angels, is pinned against the liberty of the human spirit. The UFO becomes the chariot of light, and the spirit becomes the angel. Together, they struggle to liberate the human spirit. But an Agenda from the fallen angels created the human race to entrap the human spirit, so the messenger from the light prepares to liberate the human soul by the end of the Age of Aquarius.

Therefore, man, the proposed inheritor to the human conscious, perpetrates the lie that originated from an Agenda that is created by the fallen angels. They came to earth from the 10th and 11th planets and from the 12th planet which the Sumerians called Nibiru, and they came as the result from the act of deliberate disobedience that is caused through pride.

Now, in the 21st Century, man continues to embrace the lie by employing himself to the fallacy he calls money and by living the life-style that is geared to the attainment of physical and sexual satisfaction. At the same time, man prays and he reveres human Gods in the hope to attain his perceived immortality, but the messenger, who prepares to offer man the new idea and who prepares to introduce him to the shorter path to his spiritual freedom, remains ignored.

In the 20th century, man called the messenger -- *Extraterrestrial*! He feared *E.T.*, and he cowered at the mere thought to *E.T.*'s existence. He developed misperceived and illogical concepts for the UFO and the messenger. In the 21st century, man continues to ignore and to deny the possibility the *UFO* exists. Through the motion-picture industry, he continues to mock and to ridicule the *Extraterrestrial.* He has stooped so low as to defile and to desecrate *E.T.* But above all – 21st century man continues to embrace the dark force the angels are required to protect him from, the very force that is enslaving his human spirit little by little. In view of this unknown circumstance, man remains defiant refusing to acknowledge the validity that exists behind the true UFO experience. We are left with no other recourse to take. So we have written this book for them, for the princes' of light, to acknowledge and to implore them and to allow the glorious messengers incandescent light to shine. O! Progenitor of the Universe let the glorious angels' light shine!

Therefore, you are officially introduced to the suppressed and the forgotten knowledge of the UFO and the Angel. The messenger has waited patiently for so long, and we simply cannot allow the prince of light to wait any longer. To this thought, we will say: as man masters an art or a skill, he begins from the basic level and progresses to the most complex. In the same manner, the baby begins to walk through the process of crawling.

Should man copy the baby when it comes to his belief in God? Of course he should! But does he? No he doesn't! So he derived at the preconceived notion of what the omnipotent yet mundane god shall be. But what if man approaches God through the same innocence as the little baby? He will crawl-up to the messenger from the light and know the angel is still waiting to carry him into the light and away from the darkness to place him onto the road that shall free his human spirit from the limited confines of earth's 13th dimension.

CHAPTER ONE

Beyond the Silent – Elusive – Ever-Present light

Ever since I recall, Unidentified Flying Objects have been promoting a secret and hidden agenda in my life. On my second birthday, I remember the most unbelievable and surreal moment. It was an experience that I theoretically could never imagine. Yet I distinctly remember it as though it were yesterday. There they were. I saw them as I peered out through the fifth floor living-room window. Six UFOs hovered motionlessly in the air outside the building where I lived in Spanish Harlem New York. One by one the UFOs came to stop directly in front by the window. They came to watch me. Did they know who I was?

I stood alone, captured in the awe-inspiring moment, overcome by the images that unveiled themselves before my innocent but credulous mind -- thoughts that became a part of my past memory then faded away and relocated themselves inside the storehouse of the obscure memories within the recesses of the subconscious. But the memories re-emerged many years later and introduced me to the new beginning, to the new chapter that would awaken my life. Finally! At long last! I understand what my experiences are truly destined for.

Did such an amazing experience really and truly happen to me? Did a moment so incredible become the fantasy, the memory, from a young child's dream? Not until 2008 did I begin to find the answer. Although I still treasure my special moment, I feel it belongs to a toddler's imagination. For only a far a distant and obscure memory is all that remains. But at the same time, I know deep inside the fiber of my soul, deep within the confines of my human spirit, this experience isn't to be the last encounter I will have with the UFO.

Nine and a half years passed, and I became eleven. My family and I moved from Manhattan, and we relocated ourselves in Brooklyn. One day, in the summer of 66, mom and I left New York. We boarded a Trans-Caribbean airline flight from JFK which was destined for San Juan Puerto Rico.

We arrived late the next day. Night had already fallen on the little island. Mom and I boarded a taxi from the airport and headed straight to my grandparents' house in Rio Piedras. Since the moment we arrived, the excitement within us began to mount. We were going to my grandparent's house to reunite with my brother Ruben. We would stay there for three weeks; then, mom, my brother and I, planned to return to Brooklyn. Little did Ruben, mom, and I, ever imagine, to our wildest dreams, to our wildest expectations, the excitement, the euphoria that awaited us on that unforgettable summer eve!

Ruben had been away from the city for over a year now, and I hadn't seen him in just as long of the time, so we felt content to re-kindle our newly found acquaintance. As we visited the local beaches and explored the lush tropical island, I came to feel, to re-live my roots. For the first time, in this city-boy's life, I played with iguanas, and became familiar with the sound of the native "Coqui" frog which bares its name and which became the part of the serene tropical Puerto Rican paradise.

As the weeks continued, the time arrived for us to return to Brooklyn. On the day before we were to depart, Ruben and I stayed relaxing at our grandparents' house while mom and our grandparents went shopping. Then, about three o'clock in the afternoon, when I was in the house lying on the couch watching television and Ruben was somewhere outside by the porch, he saw a UFO suddenly appear to hover some ten feet above the roof of the house.

"Smack -- whack" I heard a noise that emanated from the living room door! An astonished Ruben flings the screen door wide open and barges straight into the living-room. Instinctively, I jump up from the couch to meet him. So excited was he, Ruben couldn't express his thoughts. He is in a state of complete shock.

"Gh-gh-agh," he begins to tell me something, muttering incoherently. His mind and his lips just wouldn't comply! "Agh-gh-gh," again he tried. But his lips just wouldn't utter a single word! Ruben was speaking absolute gibberish. I became terrified to think immediately that a terrible tragedy had occurred. My heart began to pound rapidly. I felt certain something horrendous was happening outside the house and that my brother barged in to warn me about it. Since the moment he barged inside the living room, Ruben kept his finger pointing towards the door!

Within an instant or at least as far as our collective memories are concerned, Ruben and I were now standing literally stupefied within this large crowd of people. Everyone's eyes were fixated on the incredible UFO. As it flew above us, everyone fell eerily yet complacently silent. Faint whispers from the mystified crowd, coupled by the rhythmic chants from the "Coqui" frogs, echoed through the air on that serene summer eve, yet the mysterious UFO remained deafly silent as it cruised majestically by us. Shaped like an oval, it shone brighter than the full moon.

The most incredible surge of love and benevolence generated from the light; it gave me, for the moment, a significant feeling to my life. An unimaginable surge of love and uncompromised compassion stirred inside of me. I became mesmerized, captured by the light. The world seemed to implode, to shrink around my consciousness, encapsulating my spirit within the confines of the light. Time dissipated for an instant. Then I watched the silent messengers disappear slowly into the twilight sky.

At some point, Ruben and I became separated and found ourselves alone within the crowd of people, spectators who gathered to witness the once in a life-time experience. Once the excitement subsided and the crowd dissipated, we met by our grandparents' house and discovered that our mother had seen the light. Suddenly! I wasn't alone! I would return to Brooklyn with two eyewitnesses. They too saw the UFO. My mother and my brother saw the incredible silent light, the mysterious UFO that would cause me to question my physical reality forever.

Now, the months went by, and the years came, and I soon matured into a young man. About to turn 21, I enlisted in the U.S. Army in December of 1975. In August of 1977, I was sent on a tour of duty and became stationed on a military base in Okinawa Japan. About 100 soldiers came from the 155th Transportation Company in Fort Eustis, Virginia. They were brought over to fill-in for the missing Japanese workers who had gone on strike.

The soldiers lived in a barrack that was built on the beach. I stayed and shared a small room with a room-mate on the second floor. There were two windows placed on the right and on the left sides of a wall that stood across from the entrance to the room; at the front to each of them, the heads to our beds lay.

One morning I woke-up to take part in a conversation that I thought was the result of a practical joke. Evidently, my roommate vehemently insisted that while I was sleeping a bright light appeared outside of the window that stood by my bed. He felt so afraid to move or to talk from the fear of being spotted or heard by the light that he could only whisper my name. To his dismay, I never woke-up from my slumber.

That night while I slept I acted unusually strange. Although an unbearable heat and humidity was upon me, and although no cooling system was in the room, I kept myself covered from head to toe while perspiring profusely underneath the sheets, literally becoming drenched in sweat. Logic is to proceed from this experience only if the light outside the window truly occurred, for it would provide an explanation for why I behaved so unusual. Perhaps unknown to me, Ruben had interrupted the elusive pattern of the light when he had made me aware of its otherwise unknown presence. Because of my uncertainty, I didn't believe my roommate's story and remained convinced that he was playing a game on my mind. In retrospect, when I reflected on my decision, many years later, I would come to wish I had discussed the experience at some level with my roommate because it left me with a daunting and lingering doubt that returned to haunt me some 17 years later, for now my life, and my experiences with the light, would take on a whole different meaning.

New Mexico lies many thousands of miles away from Okinawa Japan and becomes separated by the Pacific Ocean literally two different worlds and two different cultures. But those two worlds and those two cultures were transformed into one when they became woven through my life through the inconspicuously-silent, purposefully-elusive, ever-present light. Within the tranquility of the Cloud Croft National Forest in New Mexico, I would become re-acquainted with the light. Once again – incredibly -- a UFO would visit me in my sleep.

On the evening of October of 1993, I boarded a bus (with my children, Evelyn, Gerry, and Erika), from the terminal in Los Angeles, California. We were en-route to Anthony, Texas to visit my in-laws Bill, Roxanne and their three children. After the long tedious ride, we arrived at the bus terminal in San Antonio Texas. I called Bill and Roxanne and they came over to pick us up. We spent a few days at their house. Then one evening, Bill decided we should go camping for a few days. Everyone agreed. The next morning we packed for the trip, and then, we boarded Bill's jeep, and he drove into New Mexico into the Cloud Croft National Forest and into his favorite Campsite.

Bill was pleased to find his favorite camping spot vacant. He pulled off the road and parked. We unloaded the camping gear and supplies from the jeep and began to pitch a tent under a large tree. The older children left to explore the campground. We adults remained to pitch the tent. When the kids returned, they told us they found a dead animal a short distance away from the campsite. Everyone went over to see it. I pressed the record button to my video camera and began to film zooming in on the carcass which was still decomposing and which had a significant stench. We walked back to the campsite wondering whether an animal or predator had attacked the elk or did it just die from natural causes.

We reached the campsite, and later on, I barbecued: hot dogs, hamburgers, and ribs. Everyone ate. Then, the kids roasted marshmallows over the campfire, and they drank hot cocoa while the adults drank hot coffee. Everyone began to chat and when it became late in the night and it became pitch black, we went inside of the tent and retired for the night. Bill and Roxanne lay in one sleeping bag to the opposite end of the tent; the kids were lying in the middle, and I lay in my sleeping bag to the other end. First, we listened to the howls that were created out in the distance by a pack of coyotes, and we talked; then, we told scary stories to each other. I fell asleep shortly after.

That morning to my complete surprise, I woke-up to relive an old and familiar theme. The time and the moment were different, and the scene and the setting had changed, but now six witnesses saw the light, and they all belong to my family. Bill and Roxanne agreed that we pitched a tent under a large tree. Sometime in the twilight, a silent light appeared above the tent and lit the inside as though it were daylight. Both of them were convinced the light hadn't come from the ground or from the sides of the tent. Bill noticed the top of the tent that had become lit was free of shadows that should have been casted down upon it from the tree that stood above. Bill and Roxanne were convinced the light didn't emanate from a helicopter because the light remained so quiet. In fact, according to both of them, everyone (with the exception of one toddler and myself sleeping inside the tent) remained so quiet they could hear themselves whisper, and aside from the vibrating sensation experienced by Roxanne not a single solitary sound came from the light. No one in the tent moved. Bill and Roxanne felt sure the inside of the tent was being observed. They became afraid. They began to feel the apprehension. What (they both feared) was about to happen next? Bill and Roxanne began to whisper my name. They hoped to wake me and alert me to the imminent danger. I remained asleep. Bill and Roxanne estimated the light had remained above the tent for approximately five minutes.

That morning Bill and Roxanne told me about the light. They explained they were afraid to move, afraid they would be heard. They began to whisper my name, yet I never woke-up. I remembered Okinawa Japan. My thoughts traversed back in time, and I compared the significant parallels between the two stories. A mind-blowing realization gripped me. Could my roommate's story have been true after all? I gathered back my senses and reasoned the parallels were caused through coincidence and removed the connection between the two experiences from my mind.

In retrospect, I would deny myself the opportunity to find the answer to my life-long mystery when I gave the two stories no further adieu. I shut down and entered into the state of denial reasoning that it would be foolish of me to entertain the absurd notion that I came into contact with beings from outer space. The thought was removed from my mind; however, a lingering doubt still remained within me about the events that transpired on that night. That morning, upon awakening, Bill and Roxanne decided that we should relocate the campsite, so we packed everything into the jeep and drove away.

October in 1994 became the first time I associated the light outside the window and the light above the tent with a UFO. Both of the experiences shared five disturbing parallels: 1. a silent light appeared; 2. witnesses observed it; 3. the witnesses were afraid to move; 4. they were reduced to a whisper; 5. I remained asleep. Although I convinced myself long ago that my roommate was joking with me, I couldn't believe that Bill and Roxanne were doing the same. So the seed of doubt became planted within my mind, and it would take 13 more years for the seed to sprout before I came to grips with the reality behind my UFO experiences.

April 22, 2008 became the turning point in my life. On that day, I acknowledged the existence of the inconspicuously-silent, purposefully-elusive, ever-present light. Although I accepted it as a part of my physical reality, I was fully cognizant that it was not a part of mans reality. On that day, I fully opened my mind to discover my true-identity, to understand my deepest, my most profound childhood moments.

I uncovered the light through the pendulum – a therapeutic device which I read about in the book entitled *Self Hypnotism* by Leslie M. McCron. I purchased the book in 1978 but never got around to reading it. For many years the book remained stored with a small selection of other books. Eighteen years passed. In 1996, I became re-acquainted with a childhood friend. He desired to read the book *Self Hypnotism*, so I gave it to him. Again the years rolled by and Dave and I lost contact. We became re-acquainted in March of 2008. One day I was in his room. My attention was drawn to a book that was filed with other books on a shelf. Something was amiss? This book stood out like a sour thumb! I reached for it. I encompassed it within my hands only to realize within seconds – this was the book I purchased in 1978! Intrigued by the moment, I asked Dave if I could take the book. He concurred. I recovered it and went on to take care of unfinished business. Did I seek, through self hypnosis, the confirmation for my UFO experiences many years ago? Perhaps! But for reasons that were unknown to me at the time but now have become perfectly clear, the endeavor was put on hold until the exact moment.

The moment came when I read chapter four from the book *Self Hypnotism*. I learned how to use the mysterious pendulum which introduced me to the subconscious. The subconscious is the part of the human psyche that man knows so little about. Since the pendulum brought me into contact with the subconscious, since the subconscious allowed me to discover my UFO experiences -- my deepest fears and my life-long suspicions were confirmed.

To my dismay, I discovered that at the age of two, then at the age of eleven, my mind was instilled with information through the subconscious. When I was a U.S. soldier in Japan, I had knowledge once again implanted inside my mind. With time, the knowledge began to slowly creep from the subconscious to my conscious causing me to reject man's written history and his disillusioned concept of reality.

Heavenly messengers rode into earth in a silent ever-present light to plant the seeds of truth within the mind's subconscious. Eventually, the seed began to sprout. As it grew, it caused me to doubt my physical reality, but the seed turned into the key that unlocked the vault, the great storehouse of forgotten knowledge that lies dormant, stagnant, within the recesses of the subconscious.

We like for you to read this book with an open and un-bias mind, so that you may shun the conditioned impulse called denial and allow us the opportunity to take you one step forward, one giant leap ahead, to take you beyond the silent – elusive – ever-present light and introduce you to the truth behind UFO, Angels and the Mayan Calendar.

CHAPTER TWO

Fall of the Seraphim Angels

Somewhere far away, on planets that lie beyond Pluto, in the outermost reaches and remote corner of the solar system – seraphim angels deserted their heavenly estates. They rebelled against the Seven Heavens -- the mandate that is created by the Progenitor of the Universe and is drafted by the archangels of the solar system, Elohim. The Seven Heavens listed two requirements the angel must follow. First, to procreate alien life the angel is required to use male and female genes from the species of an animal and to combine the genes with spirit from the angel. Secondly, the angel is required to implant the mixture inside the womb of the artificial life form.

Through the act of free will, the seraphim angels inhabited the brains of the life-forms they created by possessing their feminine and masculine bodies. One hundred percent of the Huzinite angels from the 11th Planet possessed the bodies of feminine life-forms while 100 percent of the Nephilim angels from the 12th Planet (Nibiru) and two- thirds of the angels from the 16th and 17th Planets possessed masculine ones. Since the moment they entered into the life-forms bodies, the angels' spirits fused as one with the life-forms brains, and they transgressed themselves from the incorporeal to the corporeal world.

Destined forever to exist in the corporeal state, the Nephilim and the fallen 16th and 17th Planet angels procreated alien life inside the wombs of the Huzinite. This act disobeyed the will of the Progenitor of the Universe; it disobeyed the second mandate of the Seven Heavens and started a chain-reaction through the angelic order that spread throughout the seraphim ranks.

As a result, some 200,000 years ago, the Nephilim – seraphim angels from the highest rank -- precipitated a discord that set-off the chain of events that sent shock waves shooting into space to penetrate the innermost reaches of the solar system reaching the small planet man calls earth. Somehow, the Nephilim convinced two-thirds of the seraphim ranks to procreate alien life against the second mandate of the Seven Heavens, inside the wombs of the female Huzinite; then, the Nephilim and the Huzinite climaxed the fall with their own special creation.

The order for creating alien life was listed according to the angel's native planet.

Position	Planet	Angel	Type	Fall
1st	Mercury	Raphael	Cherub	No
3rd	Earth	Elohim	Archangel	No
7th	Uranus	Melchizedek	Cherub	No
9th	Pluto	Michael	Cherub	No
11th	?	Huzin	Seraph	Yes (100%)
12th	Nibiru	Nephilim	Seraph	Yes (100%)
16th	?	?	Seraph	Yes (2/3)
17th	?	?	Seraph	Yes (2/3)

(fig. 1) Planets in the solar system with angelic life.

The younger angels were listed first; then, the older angels followed. The Seven Heavens granted first precedence to the cherubim; then, it followed with the older seraphim angels according to rank from the highest to the lowest. Mercury (the Cherub Raphael) was given the prodigious number one choice; then, the order followed: Uranus, Pluto, Nibiru, 11th, 16th, 17th Planet.

Position	1	2	3	4	5	6	7
Planet	Mercury	Uranus	Pluto	Nibiru	11th	17th	16th
Angel	Raphael	Melchizedek	Michael	Nephilim	Huzin	17th	16th

(fig. 2) Original list from the Seven Heavens.

When the moment to create alien life arrived, Raphael exercised free will and negated the opportunity to create. Because the Nephilim held fourth choice, because they are seraph of the highest rank, the 12th Planet angels anticipated on receiving the first choice, but the Seven Heavens granted first precedence to Elohim – the Archangel who held the highest rank but was the youngest among the angels.

By necessity, the first choice required Elohim to create alien life on the Planet Jupiter, but Elohim desired to create alien life on the native planet earth, so Michael, who held the third choice, obliged with the mandate to switch with Elohim.

Position	1	2	3	4	5	6	7
Planet	Earth	Uranus	Pluto	Nibiru	11th	17th	16th
Angel	Elohim	Melchizedek	Michael	Nephilim	Huzin	17th	16th

(fig. 3) Raphael drops-out. Elohim and Michael switch.

This decision did not go well with the Nephilim who were seraphim angels of the highest rank -- second only to Elohim. So the Nephilim conferred with the Seraphim order, and they waited for Michael to procreate alien life.

Michael followed with the two mandates that were required by the Seven Heavens and procreated (Ra) the alien life from Jupiter. Then, the time arrived for Melchizedek to procreate, and the cherub angel also complied by the two mandates and procreated (Viracocha) the alien life from Mars, but before Elohim could begin, the seraphim angels had rebelled against the mandate from the Seven Heavens. They wouldn't wait! Free will would overtake the spirit of the seraphim angels. Sense of pride would overcome their loyalty to the Progenitor of the Universe and convince them to rebel. Before Michael could procreate Ra, the 16th and 17th Planet angels had created alien life inside the womb of the Huzinite. Worst! The Nephilim and the Huzinite committed the abomination when they created alien life by engaging in sexual intercourse and thereby disobeyed both mandates and escalated the fall to a much higher level.

The message was relayed at once to the seraphim angels. One by one they began to fall. The Seraphim angels from the, 16th and 17th Planets were disobeying the second mandate of the Seven Heavens by procreating alien life in the womb of the Huzinite. So the domino effect began, and chaos ensued in the solar system.

When the Nephilim, the Huzinite, the 16th and the 17th Planet angels fell from their angelic states, their spirits did so by possessing the physical bodies which they had created, and when the fall occurred, it started on the Planet Saturn. There the Huzinite was donating her womb for the 16th and the 17th Planet fallen angels to procreate alien life in. After the fall of the 16th and 17th Planet angels, the Nephilim followed the Huzinite to Saturn. There they created the Seven Headed Serpent by engaging in sexual intercourse and thereby further defied the Seven Heavens.

Enoch, the great grandfather of Noah, the seventh from Adam, provides the glimpse into that obscure moment in time when the Nephilim committed yet another abomination. So close to God, was he; the Bible foretold that he went to heaven without experiencing physical death. There, according to Enoch, he wrote several books. One in particular, *the Book of Enoch* emerges from the chambers of antiquity to proclaim its true authenticity. By the most conservative estimate, a copy of the book, which is found with the dead-sea scrolls, dates at 2 B.C., and its source is thought to be some 3,000 years old; thus, the book is old, and we contend that it provides the account of a group of Nephilim angels that arrive on earth some 9,000 years ago.

Enoch chapter seven, verses one thru seven, "It happened after the sons of men had multiplied in those days, that daughters were born to them, elegant and beautiful. And when the angels, the sons of heaven [the Nephilim], beheld them, they became enamoured of them, saying to each other, Come, let us select for ourselves wives from the progeny of men, and let us beget children. Then their leader Samyaza said to them; I fear that you may perhaps be indisposed to the performance of this enterprise; And that I alone shall suffer for so grievous a crime. But they answered him and said; We all swear; And bind ourselves by mutual execrations, that we will not change our intention, but execute our projected undertaking. Then they swore all together, and all bound themselves by mutual execrations. Their whole number was two hundred, who descended upon Ardis, which is the top of mount Armon."

Some nine thousand years ago Enoch became a messenger between the Nephilim (who were wrecking havoc on earth) and the biblical God. Not only had the Nephilim created the fall, not only had the Nephilim and Isis created the Seven Headed Serpent in Saturn, but now, some 190,000 years later, the Nephilim would create the giants on earth (Enoch 7:11-12), "And the women conceiving brought forth giants. Whose stature was each 300 cubits."

We acquire a glimpsc at the severity of the transgressions that are committed by the Nephilim when God [Elohim] speaks (Enoch 15:1-7), "...O righteous Enoch, thou scribe of righteousness: approach hither, and hear my voice. Go, say to the Watchers of heaven [Nephilim], who have sent thee to pray for them, You ought to pray for men, and not men for you. Wherefore have you forsaken the lofty and holy heaven, which endures forever, and have lain with women; have defiled yourselves with the daughters of men; have taken to yourselves wives; have acted like the sons of the earth, and have begotten an impious offspring? You being spiritual, holy, and possessing a life which is eternal, have polluted yourselves with women; have begotten in carnal blood; have lusted in the blood of men; and have done as those who are flesh and blood do. These however die and perish. But you from the beginning were made spiritual, possessing a life which is eternal, and not subject to death forever. Therefore, I made not wives for you, because, being spiritual, your dwelling is in heaven."

The verses from the book of Enoch make it perfectly clear. In order to understand the significance of the fall, we need to understand the incorporeal nature of the angel. They are composed from a body of light and guided by the mind of pure thought. Angels are the beings of light that emerge from within the accounts of the near death experience. The biblical angel like the spirit inside the UFO is associated with the presence of a bright light, and the spirit, like the angel, cannot establish physical contact with a human subject.

Since the angel comes from the incorporeal world, the spirit can only make contact with the mind. Due to the forces that govern the universe, physical contact between an angel and a human is impossible. In the Bible, whenever the angel appears in the physical-form we are assured the angel is a Nephilim, and whenever the angel appears in the light-form, we are assured it is the spirit. When the fallen angels chose to disobey the will of the Progenitor of the Universe, they did so inside the bodies of the special life-forms they had created, so their actions did not go without a consequence because the fall changed their incorporeal nature into the corporeal state.

Thus, 170,000 years ago, Elohim instructed Gabriel to remove the fallen seraphim angels from the earth for violating the two mandates of the Seven Heavens; the 16th and 17th Planet angels complied at once, and they handed themselves over to Gabriel. They were removed from the earth and are presently confined within the 15th dimension in their respective planets. Six hundred and sixty-six thousand Nephilim and 666,000 Huzinite hid themselves on the earth within the 13th dimension. The remaining 333,000 Nephilim and 333,000 Huzinite turned themselves over to Gabriel. Thus, two-thirds of the Nephilim and two-thirds of the Huzinite refused to comply with the conditions that were set forth for their surrender, so they remained on earth to be destined to move from planet to planet.

Consequently, some 9,000 years ago, the Nephilim and the Huzinite fled Mars to once again come to earth. Six hundred sixty-six thousand Nephilim settled by modern day Israel and established the ancient city of Resen; they became renown to the prehistoric world as El -- the god of earthly procreation.

(fig.4) Ancient Figurine depicting El.

Six hundred sixty-six thousand Huzinite settled near the Tigris River and created the civilization of ancient Mesopotamia. The Huzinite would become renown to the prehistoric world as Isis -- the Egyptian goddess of fertility. Now, the Seven Headed Serpent followed.

(fig.5) Ancient figurine shows Isis holding the Seven Headed Serpent.

The group settled by the Euphrates River and created the civilization of ancient Sumer.

One hundred seventy thousand years ago two different pantheon of gods arrived on earth. One group (Ra) came to prepare Michael and Elohim for the creation of alien life; the other, the Nephilim and the Huzinite, came as a consequence to the fall. Together, they became responsible for supplying the genes that created the first family of the human race. One hundred seventy thousand years ago the Nephilim and the Huzinite, would set into motion the chain of events that ultimately shaped and determined how the human race evolved.

CHAPTER THREE

Creation of the Human Race

It has long been written within the book of Genesis and within the book of Enoch that two separate falls occurred on earth. The Mayan calendar highlights the fall of the Seraphim angels which occurred about 200,000 years ago, and it is from this time-frame that we will start to recount man's story. On earth, some 170,000 years ago, the newly crowned god (Ra) had arrived to assist Elohim and Michael with the creation of alien life. Ra came to earth to create the special life-form which is needed for the procreation. The group settled in the geographic region that is called Cairo Egypt to leave a legacy behind that has survived to this 21st century. The newly crowned god (Viracocha) also arrived from Mars to complete the pantheon of gods that first came to planet earth.

Amiss the newly found chaos and the newly created turmoil which ensued after the biblical fall, Elohim and Michael were preparing to create alien life according to the time-frame from the Seven Heavens.

So commenced the primordial beginning to the human race proliferating itself within the backdrop of the jungles in South Africa. There the Australopithecine species

(fig.6) Australopithecus Africanus

roamed in the wild Ra had observed them and planned to use their genes for the creation of Malek – the special life-form with the spirit of consciousness that is on the schedule for donating the womb that is needed for the procreation. But before Ra could use the Australopithecines, Michael descended to earth to prepare the apes for the creation. Michael removed genes from the female and the male Australopithecines and implanted the genes with spirit then handed them over to Ra.

When the specific time for the creation arrived, Ra mixed the male and female genes from the Australopithecines, which contained the Michael spirit, with genes of an alien from Jupiter and implanted the mixture inside the womb of the artificial life-form. Then Ra waited for the allotted period for labor to elapse. Ten months later emerged the prototype to the Neanderthal species – female Homo Habilis. She resembled the great ape and measured between six to seven feet. Habilis was strong and muscular. She weighed approximately four hundred pounds. Although she was created to be the prototype to the creation of the Malek species, Habilis was biologically a female and could reproduce through sexual intercourse.

Next, Ra removed genes from Habilis; Ra repeated the procedure to create Neanderthal. By definition she was anatomically female, but by specificity, Neanderthal couldn't reproduce through sexual intercourse. She measured between four and one-half to five feet, and she weighed approximately one hundred twenty pounds. Neanderthal would be considered petite according to today's standards. Her most remarkable feature was her "big buttock." Since she didn't inherit the Michael spirit, Neanderthal came to be depicted to the ancient world as a pregnant and faceless or decapitated female.

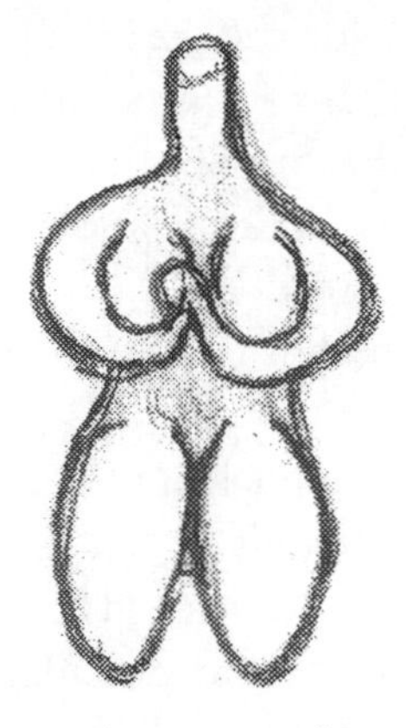

(Fig. 7) Female statuette from Samarra
6000 BC
Headless female Neanderthal

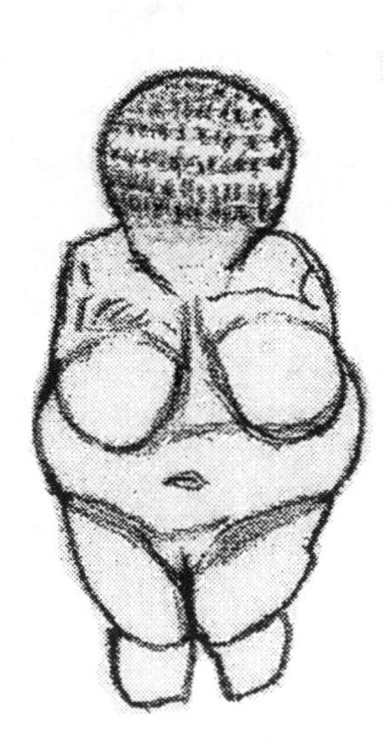

(Fig. 8) Venus of Willendorf
25000 BC
Faceless pregnant female Neanderthal.

Contrary to what history teaches, Neanderthal didn't become extinct: she went to Venus some 160,000 thousand years ago to be used for reproduction.

Now, as the moment for the creation of Malek drew near. Ra mixed genes of Neanderthal with genes of an alien from Jupiter and repeated the procedure. Again, the allotted period for labor elapsed. Ten months later emerged Malek – known to the ancient world as Adapa and to the modern world as the biblical Adam.

The creation story, which is found in Genesis 1:27, informs man of this huge and stupendous moment, "So God [Ra] created man [Malek] in his own image [gene] in the image of God [Ra's DNA] created he him; male and female [a pair] created he them."

Feminine and masculine Malek had frizzy black hair and a purple black skin complexion. Both were muscular and measured between five to six feet. Since the moment they were created, feminine and masculine Malek were separated so they wouldn't breed. Since both acquired no human spirit, they possessed no thought; however, Malek possessed the spirit for consciousness.

To culminate the creation, Ra created Homo-Erectus through a gene mix from Pluto and Habilus. He was massive and impressive and resembled the great ape. Erectus stood seven and one-half to eight feet tall and weighed approximately four hundred fifty pounds. Erectus and Habilis mated to create Bigfoot. On earth, some 9,000 years ago, Bigfoot supplied the labor for the construction of the Sphinx and for the three great pyramids in Giza, for Stonehedge in Great Britain and for Teotihuacan and Sacsahuaman in Peru. The descendants that came from the offspring of Habilis and Erectus made possible the myths and the legends that surround the Bigfoot, the Sasquash, and the Yeti creatures.

Although man has led himself to believe that he is rooted to Cro-Magnon (Homo-Erectus), his roots are to Neanderthal. Erectus owed his lineage to Habilis, but he was never used in the creation of the human race. Erectus was specifically created to produce the big-foot specie, and he and Habilis produced the Bigfoot race. Homo-Sapian owed his lineage to Malek who owed its lineage to female Neanderthal and not to Erectus, and she owed her lineage to the Australopithecine ape.

Neanderthal's sole purpose became her womb, and Erectus's sole purpose became his semen. She was created specifically to breed offspring; he was created specifically to produce. Neanderthal would breed Malek within her womb, yet her womb couldn't reproduce through sexual intercourse. Erectus produced Bigfoot within the womb of Habilis through sexual intercourse. Therefore, we have come to conclude: Neanderthal was note a brute. She was a special creation that served to reproduce the special life-form – the Malek species -- while Habilis and Erectus served solely as prototypes.

One hundred and seventy thousand years ago when the Nephilim and the Huzinite fell to earth Malek had not yet been created. However, after the Malek species emerged, the Nephilim and the Huzinite immediately invented the breeding ritual. On earth, the ritual began as the attempt to locate male Malek so to gather their semen; then, the genes from Malek and the spirit from El could be combined within a mixture and implanted inside the Huzinite's womb to procreate the offspring. Masculine Malek was living in what is now Central Africa in the ancient city of Calneh. He lived inside a sheltered dwelling that was located on the top of Mount Horeb where he waited to unite with feminine Malek after the procreation of alien life.

The Huzinite was to follow with another ritual: physically mate with the Sons of God; they were the special life-forms that are created by Elohim that are on the schedule to donate genes that will be implanted inside of the wombs of Malek to procreate alien life on the earth. Like Malek, the Sons of God had acquired no thought; however, they too possessed the spirit for consciousness. Created inside the Garden of Eden, they stood ten feet tall and weighed approximately 220 pounds. four hundred and forty-six thousand Sons of God were created in just 40 days.

Meanwhile, the Huzinite exited the geographic region that is Canaan – an ancient land bridge that once connected the continents that are Africa, Asia, and Europe – and entered into the city of Calneh. They began ascending Mount Horeb. When they reached a certain point, the Huzinite encountered the Sons of God. Some of them enticed the Sons of God and lured them to engage in sexual intercourse; the other ones continued to ascend to the top of the Mount to search for masculine Malek.

So important became the first attempt to breed the human-race that the story immediately follows the six days of creation. Genesis chapter six, verses 1-2 tells the story, "It came to pass when men [the incarnated Nephilim] began to multiply on the face of the earth and daughters [the incarnated Huzinite] were born [brought] unto them. That the Sons of God saw the daughters of men that they were fair; and they took them wives of all which they chose." These verses become consistent with the first fall on the earth when the Nephilim and the Huzinite interrupt the creation of alien life by mating with the Sons of God.

Genesis 6:4 continues the story, "There were giants [the incarnated Nephilim] in the earth in those days [before the mating happens]; and also after that, when the Sons of God came in unto the daughters of men, and they bare children to them." Verse four delineates the moment when the Nephilim, who had concocted the scheme for the Huzinite to mate with the Sons of God in the first place, were placed physically on the earth before and also after the breeding ritual occurs; thus, the verse indirectly corroborates the understanding the Nephilim and the Huzinite share that seeks to carry-out a secret and a covert agenda.

The Sons of God (Genesis 6:1), who are created by Elohim, should never become confused with the Sons of Heaven (Enoch 7:2) who are the very Nephilim incarnate. These two accounts entail falls which occurred on two separate periods of time. The biblical verse in Genesis 6:4 combines these two accounts into one story; it begins with the story of the biblical Sons of God who fell some 171,000 years ago when alien life was on the schedule to occur on earth, and ends with the story from Enoch 7:2 which describes a more recent fall, one that occurred a mere 9,000 years ago when the Nephilim (now known as El) degenerated to the lowest of levels by cohabiting with feminine Malek.

Genesis 6:4 explained both accounts through one story. Later on, some 3,000 years ago, the editors of the book of Enoch used the Sons of Heaven story, and the editors of the book of Genesis used the story of the Sons of God. Although the immense difference of 162,000 years separates both accounts, as we will find out in chapter six, to the angel, it stands for exactly 16.2 days of celestial time. Man's oldest myths, his most venerated and sacred sagas – are written through the guise of celestial time, for what appears as a day for the gods stands as thousands and thousands of years for man.

Therefore, one hundred seventy-one thousand years ago the ritual produced the hybrid creation which we will call the Nation of Israel, a mixture from the special life-form that was created by Elohim and the Huzinite. The male stood ten to eleven feet tall. He weighed approximately two hundred and thirty pounds. He had straight black hair and a dark brown complexion. The male from the Nation of Israel served one purpose for the Nephilim and for the Huzinite: to be strictly a prototype people.

Meanwhile, the remaining Huzinite continued to climb Mount Horeb until they reached the top of the summit. They called-out for masculine Malek. Nearly two days passed by as the Huzinite played music and danced provocatively in the hope to lure them outside. Malek's masculine prowess was aroused, and Malek strongly desired to go outside, but the 144,000 (un-fallen) Sons of God kept them locked and secured. After the breeding ordeal was over, 302,000 Sons of God fell to the breeding ritual but masculine Malek was spared.

Since the scheme to acquire the semen from Malek failed, the Nephilim and the Huzinite accused Elohim of interfering with the breeding ritual. Consequently, 170,000 years ago the first conflict in the solar system commenced as a war that began on earth that caused the Nephilim and the Huzinite to flee and to begin to move from planet to planet until they arrived back on earth some 9,000 years ago, a war that was precipitated by pride and was commandeered by the fallen angels. But the moment, the battle, the glory, belonged to the angel Michael. Now – on with man's story!

To prevent feminine and masculine Malek from falling prey to the breeding ritual, Ra decided to unite them. Genesis chapter one, verse twenty eight commemorates this momentous and historic moment, "Then God [Ra] blessed them, and God said to them, be fruitful and multiply, replenish, the earth." So the Malek species flourished uninterrupted for one hundred fifty thousand years.

Several thousand years passed since the Malek species flourished as the diplomatic tensions between Ra and the Seven Headed Serpent reached the all-time high. Both were battling each other for the control of vital geographic regions on the different planets. Through diplomacy, some 164,000 years ago, the Seven Headed Serpent gained control; however, this development became short lived because within just a mere 14,000 thousand years Ra would regain the hold. This last diplomatic victory escalated the tensions between them even higher and would bring them to the un-paralleled level that culminated in a war that pinned Ra against the Seven Headed Serpent.

Some 150,000 years ago, on the Tenth Planet, the Nephilim and the Huzinite (knowing that a war was about to begin) genetically manipulated their own genes and through the womb of the Huzinite procreated the Kenizzite people. The male Kenizzite had a light brown skin complexion and had straight black hair. He stood five to five and one-half feet tall and weighed approximately 200 pounds. The Kenizzite people acquired a significant fold in the position of both eyes. This feature, which was observed foremost in the Seven Headed Serpent, is caused from mixing two special life-forms with angelic spirit – the Nephilim and the Huzinite. In the 21st century A.D., the Kenizzite features are better distinguished within the Asian and the Chinese races.

Consequently, throughout the different times, and the different planets, war waged in the solar system between Ra and the Seven Headed Serpent for about 126,000 years. Then, on the Planet Jupiter, some 26,000 years ago, a situation arose that set the stage for the emergence of the human race. Because of the devastation the war created, the dwellings of Bigfoot and the dwellings of Malek were destroyed. This mishap caused a calamitous situation that left Bigfoot and Malek stranded without shelter. Originally, the Bigfoot species was created in the southern part of the continent which is Africa. There they were taught and were instructed by Viracocha, but later, Ra removed them from the earth, and they eventually would arrive on Jupiter some 26,000 years ago.

Although Ra responded immediately to the crisis and recovered eighty per cent of the feminine and masculine Malek, the Seven Headed Serpent seized the moment and recovered the other twenty percent along with a small number of the Bigfoot species. Now, through the acquisition of Malek, the breeding ritual escalated one level higher when genes from the Amorite (recovered feminine Malek) were mixed with spirit from the Nephilim and became implanted inside the womb of the Huzinite. Nine months later the ancient Egyptian was born.

The Babylonian epic of creation the Enuma Elish (which dates to 1,000 B.C.) shares a glimpse into that obscure moment in time when the ancient Egyptian people were procreated (tablet 6:5-8), "Blood [spirit] will I form and cause bone to be; Then will I set up my *lullu*, 'Man' shall be his name! Yes, I will create *lullu*: Man! (Upon him) shall the services of the gods be imposed that they may be at rest."

Some 26,000 years ago, the Nephilim and the Huzinite procreated the ancient Egyptian people so that the ancient Egyptian people can service and provide them with their physical needs. Therefore, the word worship has now to take on this whole new and different meaning, for it implies the ancient Egyptian people were created specifically to service the needs of the fallen incarnate angels.

In a tablet from the first Babylonian Dynasty which concerns itself with the creation of man, we read (third column lines 22-27), "Let them slay a god, And let the gods.... With his [man's] flesh and his [a god's] blood Let Ninhursag mix clay. God and man .... united(?) in the clay." Although the remaining lines are so badly damaged that they are no longer legible, the spirit nature of man becomes established through the use of the word blood which is mixed with man's genes (flesh) and a god's spirit (blood) and combined in a clay-like substance.

The ancient Egyptian had dark-brown frizzy hair and a dark-brown complexion. The male measured six to six and one-half feet. He weighed approximately two hundred fifty pounds. As we examine the difference between the genetic line of the Kenizzite and the genetic line of the ancient Egyptian people, we will discover that the Kenizzite derived from the mix of a fallen incarnate Nephilim and an incarnate Huzinite angel, but the Egyptian derived from the mix of a fallen incarnate Huzinite angel and the Malek specie.

This distinct yet related difference between the Kenizzite gene and the ancient Egyptian produced the two respective lines of Cain and of Seth and echoed the breeding ritual in the sexual escapades that are found contained within the ancient Sumerian tales of Innana and her two half brothers Enki and Enlil which Author Zacaria Sitchin has meticulously disclosed in his series of books known as the *Earth Chronicles.*

His deciphering of the Sumerian tablets (excavated from 1848-1876 by Layard, Rassam, and Smith) brought Sitchin to document the Annunaki's (the Nephilim and the Huzinite's) history since the fall, and it brought him to document the involvement they both shared in the breeding ritual on earth. The ritual, which is being conducted by the Sumerian goddess Innana (a Huzinite), used her womb to procreate a legitimate heir to the throne for her two half-brothers Enki and Enlil. Enki was an ancient Egyptian who came from the womb of Malek, and Enlil was a Kenizzite who came from the womb of the Huzinite. Enki belonged to the line of Seth and Enlil belonged to the line of Cain, and they both shared the spirit of Michael and competed between themselves to produce the legitimate heir to the throne. Sitchin demonstrated this same relationship in the book of Genesis within the story of Sarah and her half-brother Abraham. This half-sister and half-brother relationship will be discussed in the next chapter.

Once Malek became a part of the breeding ritual, Elohim invited a group of the cherubim angels to come to the Planet Mars. Melchizedek departed first from the Planet Uranus; Michael left Pluto to follow, and Raphael departed last from the Planet Mercury. Sixteen thousand years ago they established a settlement on the area of Mars that scientists call Cydonia. The sole purpose for the angels' visit became the breeding ritual that would soon turn out of control. No longer was it going to be necessary for the Nephilim and the Huzinite to isolate the gene of Malek to use in the breeding ritual. Now, the newly created ancient Egyptian people and the older Kenizzite people could be conditioned to breed on their own.

Once again, the drama quickly shifted when the Nephilim (El), the Huzinite (Isis), and the Seven Headed Serpent (Satan) escaped to earth. Elohim followed them and created a Garden for the angels to reside in Mesopotamia. Melchizedek lived by the Pison River in the city of Havilah. Michael, by the Gihon River in Ethiopia, and Raphael lived by the Hiddekel River in Assyria; in addition, the Garden strategically lay near the Euphrates River. There the laboratory for breeding the human race lay in Canaan.

Despite the presence of the angels in the garden, the breeding ritual was transformed into a mating ritual. About 7,645 years ago (determined by adding the ages of the 10 patriarchs minus Adam's age or 8575 – 930), Cain, the male Kenizzite, was put to breed with the ancient female Egyptian (Seth) for 105 years to produce the Kenite (Enos) by 5529 B.C. The Kenite had dark-brown hair and a brown complexion. The female Kenite measured four and a half to five feet and weighed approximately one hundred thirty pounds.

Soon thereafter, the Canaanite (Cainan) emerged by 5439 B.C. The Canaanite was produced by breeding the male Egyptian (Seth) with the female Enos for 90 years. The male Canaanite had frizzy black hair and a black complexion. He measured six and a half to seven feet and weighed approximately two hundred fifty pounds. Specifically, the Kenite people and the Canaanite race originate from the line of Seth, the ancient Egyptian genetic line which according to the book of Genesis descends from Adam.

The Hittite (Enoch) emerged by 5400 B.C. as the resultant breed between the male Cain and the female Enos. The Hittite had curly brown hair and a brown complexion. She measured from five to five and one-half feet and weighed approximately one hundred twenty pounds.

Two hundred years later (Irad) the Jebusite emerged. A breed between the male Cainan and the female Enoch, the Jebusite had straight dark-brown hair and a light-brown complexion. The female measured four and a half to five feet and weighed approximately one hundred ten pounds. Specifically, the Hittite and the Jebusite races originated from the line of Cain, the genetic line that descends from the Kenizzite people.

After he is banished from the Garden of Eden (Genesis 4:17-19) reports, "Cain knew his wife; and she conceived, and bare Enoch: and he builded a city, and called the name of the city, after the name of his son, Enoch. And unto Enoch was born Irad: and Irad begat Mehujael: and Mehujael begat Methusael: and Methusael begat Lamech."

Isn't it true the names Cain, Enoch, and Lamech are also listed in the line of Seth as Cainan, Enoch, and Lamech, and is it a coincidence the names Mehujael and Methusael that derive from the line of Cain are very similar in meaning to the ones Mahalaleel and Methuselah that derive from the line of Seth. Certainly, the mating ritual began just after the biblical flood ended, and the names that are identical to both of the lines end with Lamech who was the father of Noah. This fact leads us to propose the idea that Cain, Enoch, and Lamech were the same group of people that existed contemporaneously as half-brothers within the two lines. Their names chronologically appear just before the biblical flood after the mating ritual began.

Line of Seth	Line of Cain
(4th born Cainan)	(8th born Tubal-cain)
(7th born Enoch)	(1st born Enoch)
(9th born Lamech)	(5th born Lamech)
(5th born Mahalaleel)	(3rd born Mehujael)
(8th born Methuselah)	(4th born Methusael)

(fig. 9) Similarity between the names of the descendants from both lines.

In addition, the name of Enoch coincides with the appearance of the solar calendar while the name of Lamech coincides with the appearance of the biblical flood. If this contention becomes true, it hints to the connection that exists between the breeding ritual and the solar calendar, for it was after Enoch leaves earth that the solar calendar was implemented and the mating ritual began.

About 7,000 years ago, Gabriel requested to El and Isis to surrender and they finally did. Handing themselves over to the Cherub Gabriel, El and Isis were sequestered within the Garden, and it seemed the breeding ritual would come to the halt. The story in Genesis 6:5 explains what happened next, "And God [the forces of nature] saw that the wickedness [degradation] of man was great in the earth, and that every imagination of the thoughts of his heart was only evil continually."

So the biblical flood ensues (Genesis 7:11-12), "In the six hundredth year of Noah's life, in the second month, the seventeenth day of the month, the same day were all the fountains of the great deep (polar ice-caps) broken up, and the windows of heaven were opened. And the rain was upon the earth forty days and forty nights."

The biblical flood now in progress, the breeding ritual terminated, El and Isis sequestered within the Garden – brought the Seven Headed Serpent to create an alliance with El and Isis. This long lasting alliance would become the final and desperate attempt to create the human race. Therefore, from this point forward, the alliance formed by the three groups will be called an Agenda of a Snake.

Now, the frequency, the intensity, of the mating ritual accelerated to take an incredibly rapid pace. Four races emerged within a mere 200 years. In Central America, the Seven Headed Serpent arranged for the creation of the Kadmonite (Afro-Asiatic) and the Perizzite (Chinese) races. In 4500 B.C., the Kadmonite race emerged as a breed between the female Hittite and the male Canaanite. The Kadmonite had frizzy brown hair and a brown complexion. The male measured, upright, about six feet and weighed approximately two hundred twenty pounds. The Perizzite race emerged as a breed between the female Hittite and the male Jebusite. The Perizzite had straight black hair and a light-brown complexion. The female measured from four to four and one-half feet and weighed approximately 105 pounds.

At the time the Seven Headed Serpent created the Kadmonite race, the group was also creating the male Hebrew race near the Caucus Mountains. The male from the Nation of Israel (Shem) was put to breed with the female Amorite for five hundred years to produce the Hebrew (Terah). In 4500 B.C., the male Hebrew emerged. He measured five to six feet tall and weighed approximately 230 pounds. The male Hebrew had straight black hair and a dark brown complexion.

Nine hundred years passed. The Seven Headed Serpent was breeding the male Hebrew with the female Amorite. By 3600 B.C., the male Israelite emerged. He measured five to six feet and weighed approximately two hundred and thirty pounds. He had dark brown hair and a light brown complexion. The male Israelite was placed on the schedule to breed with the descendant of the Amorite but was prevented from doing so by the angels in the garden.

Since the Israelite descended from the Hebrew, since the Hebrew held the status of being the chosen people, we should define what it means to be an Israelite or a Hebrew. The Israelite was a descendant from the Hebrew who descended from the Nation of Israel, so the Israelite derived from a species alien to the human race. The Jew didn't descend from the Israelite because the Israelite was genetically linked to the Hebrew who was genetically linked to The Nation of Israel, and they were genetically rooted to the fallen Sons of God and Isis. The Jew was genetically linked to the Afro-Asiatic race that was genetically rooted to Malek. Once Elohim realized the claim the Hebrews' made, Elohim instilled into the 144,000 (un-fallen) Sons of God the Elohim spirit bequeathing them with the status as Elohim's chosen people.

Finally, some 6,000 years ago, acting under the request that came from the Archangel Elohim, Gabriel ended the angels stay in the garden and requested they should leave earth. Ra went back to reside within the first dimension on the Planet Jupiter. Viracocha went to reside within the first dimension on Deimos – a moon of Mars. Melchizedek and Raphael also went to reside within the first dimensions in their respective planets. The request was made by the Israelites to stay on earth's 13th dimension and to inherit the kingship, the wealth, and the power they enjoyed, but it was denied to them, so they went to live within the fifth dimension on the Planet Nibiru.

Now, on earth Gabriel confined El and Isis to the 15th and the 14th dimensions, respectively, and the Seven Headed Serpent stood confined to the eighth dimension under the earth: to be reckoned with on the Day of Judgment. The Seven Headed Serpent plus El and Isis will suffer the ill consequences for their untimely deeds.

The ancient concept of hell commenced when the Seven Headed Serpent became confined to the eighth dimension under the earth. The concept of Satan originates from the Seven Headed Serpent whose seven heads represents the position of the Planet Saturn when counting in the direction from the Twelve Planet (Nibiru) coming toward the sun. Therefore, the name Satan derives its roots from the Planet Saturn which originally bared Satan's name. The depiction of Satan derived from the appearance of the reptilian-type skin of the Seven Headed Serpent which was genetically predisposed to the bodies of the biological life-forms the Nephilim and the Huzinite possessed.

So the final stages for the creation of the human race was put into place, but as we will discover in chapter four, there is a purpose, a reason, an underlying motive for the mating ritual, and it involves itself around the creation of a predetermined people that will forever change the course of human history.

CHAPTER FOUR

Agenda of a Snake

By 4500 B.C., the long forgotten agenda -- an Agenda of a Snake – is being enforced onto the Human people. An ancient mating ritual has been imposed onto the newly created Huzin-man race. To be orchestrated by El and Isis, the ritual is to be commandeered by their special creation -- the Seven Headed Serpent.

Now with the spirits of El and Isis confined to earth's 14th and 15th dimensions, the Seven Headed Serpent accelerated the pace of the ritual transforming it into a desperate but successful attempt to create the human race. But at the final outcome, the mating ritual was to go haywire and to turn completely out of control by 600 B.C.

In the spotlight, appearing in center stage to the ancient melodrama stood feminine Malek. A descendant of Homo Habilis then of Neanderthal, the Malek species owed its lineage to the Australopithecine. Malek was a member of the ape-kingdom. The Malek species was the highest member in the animal kingdom and like the animals, feminine and masculine Malek were created as a pair. They held supremacy over the whole animal kingdom. Feminine and masculine Malek were the special life-form possessing alien lineage to Ra.

Since Malek belongs to the animal kingdom, it possessed consciousness. After all! Doesn't any member of the animal kingdom possess consciousness? Well -- Malek is to be no exception! An Agenda of a Snake became keenly aware of this. Consciousness can be defined as spirit: a special awareness or sensitivity. Spirit becomes the manner in which the animal can become aware and sensitive to the three-dimensional world. By using the five senses – sight, hearing, touch, taste, smell – the animal sorts out then understands the external stimuli it receives from the physical world.

One question submerges to the conscious surface of the mind: why did an Agenda breed the line of Cain with the line of Seth? What motive, what purpose, could there be for the human to serve an Agenda of a Snake? Once more, we are reminded: the Nephilim and the Huzin angel possessed the biological bodies of the special life-forms that they were mandated to procreate alien life in; then, they bequeathed into them their spirits. Well, in the case for the human being, Isis donated her womb to provide the spirit that became necessary to create the human body, and then through an Agenda, she donated, first, the womb from the descendants of the line of Cain and then the womb from the descendants of the line of Seth to breed the human race.

In the final analysis, the experiment was intended to advance an agenda that became enforced through a predetermined chosen people. Now -- we have disclosed the truth! An Agenda of a Snake chose to create a people with an El and Isis spirit and consciousness because it planned to create then to later control the mind of the human being.

But why did an Agenda require feminine Malek? Simply, because Malek belongs to the animal kingdom, so its offspring possessed the capacity to give birth to a race with the propensity to develop consciousness, and then, this race would give rise to a people with a conscious. An agenda knows one hundred percent, once the human brain developed consciousness, the human conscious would be created through the scientific manipulation of alien and human genes.

This dual nature – to possess the capacity to develop consciousness and to acquire the propensity to develop the human conscious – forms the prerequisite for an Agenda's mating ritual. The prerequisite involves itself around the fact that a brain with an El or Isis spirit and consciousness will develop the human conscious. An Agenda's purpose has been revealed! Now -- it is perfectly clear! A descendant from Malek, who develops the human conscious, is what an Agenda sought all along.

In the subsequent chapter, much will be said about man's spirit and the human conscious, but in order for us to continue with this present discussion on the human race, it will become necessary to understand that an Agenda created the Huzin-man (the 2nd family) by scientifically manipulating genes from the Kennizite (the line of Cain) and genes from Malek (the line of Seth); then, an Agenda put to breed the descendants from the both lines to create the human race.

As we revealed in chapter three, the human race originates from the mixture of genes that came from the oldest most revered Gods of the ancient world -- Isis, Ra, El. To no surprise, had we come to uncover the true meaning behind the name Israel, for it implies much more than the simple meaning which is being attributed to it. Israel implies the names of the three gods who in Canaan, some 9,000 years ago, became responsible for the first generation of the human race to emerge.

The first generation – the generation of Is-Ra-El -- according to mythological folklore arrived from the heavens. Here-upon whenever someone speaks-out the name Israel, he or she will be invoking the memory of the first generation of the human race; the memory of Isis who donated her special womb; Ra who unwillingly donated, through Malek, the capacity for consciousness; El who donated the propensity for the human conscious.

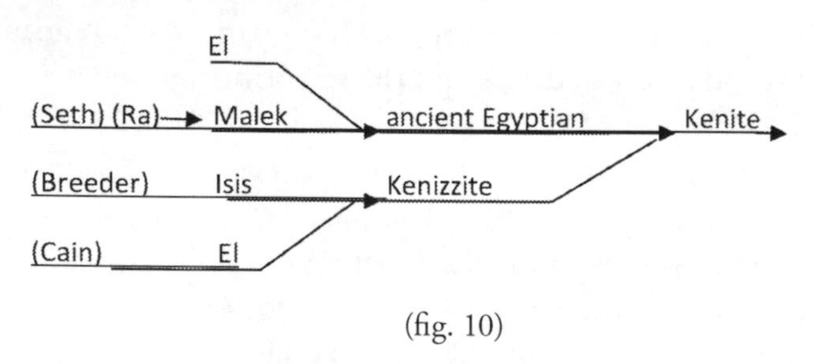

(fig. 10)

Thus, the Huzin family (the second family of the human race) came from a mix of three genes; one gene through El originates from Nibiru (the 12th Planet); the second, through Isis, originates from the 11th Planet; the third, through Malek, originates from the Planet Pluto. Through genetic manipulation of the three genes, an Agenda produced three genetically related groups of people from which two male groups (Egyptian and Kenizzite) and one female group (Kenite) were designated for breeding.

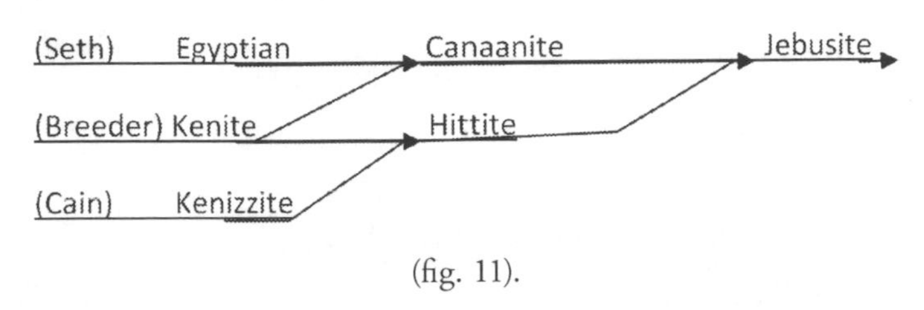

(fig. 11).

The larger female Kenite group was divided into two separate groups; one group was put to breed with the group of male Egyptians, and the other, with the group of male Kenizzites to bring forth the two distinct but related groups called the Canaanite and Hittite races. Then, at the appropriate time, the male group from the Canaanite race and the female group from the Hittite race were put to breed with one another to produce the third group called the Jebusite race. Consequently, the three acquired racial groups formed the third family for the third generation. The third family shared the same three genes but in different percentages. In such manner, the families of the human race emerged.

The Four biblical Generations

First Generation (Israel)

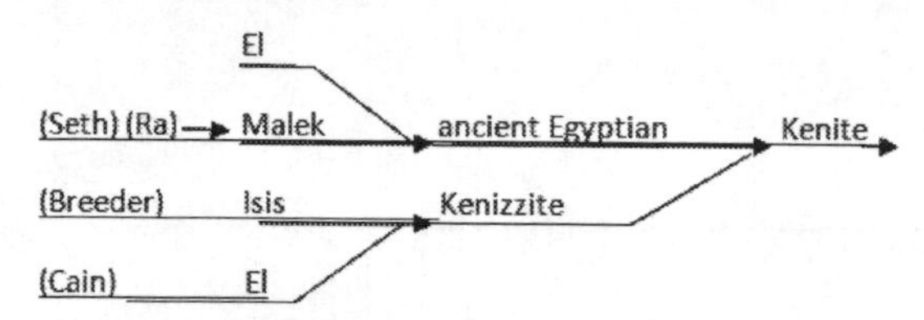

Second Generation (Noah)

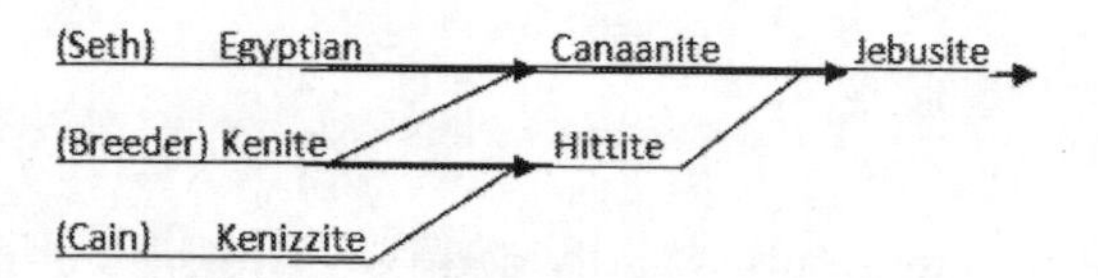

Third Generation (Abram)

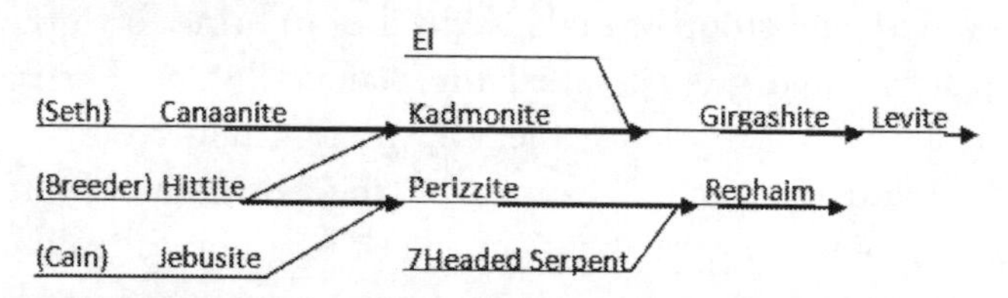

Fourth Generation (Abraham)

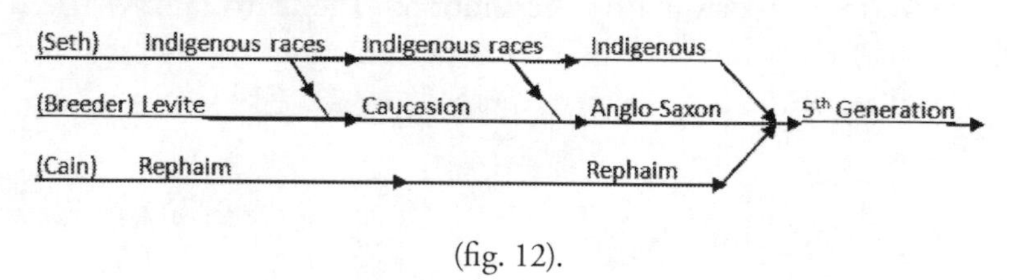

(fig. 12).

The family, as is delineated in the book of Genesis, brought forth the subsequent generation. The Bible refers to the generation through the name of a biblical patriarch, and each patriarch consists of a family that is composed from the three races that are genetically related.

It is important to note that for the first 800 years since it is written the Old Testament went through a series of edits. In the book of Genesis, some chapters are interwoven to give the appearance that a patriarch existed for an enormous length of time, but this simply isn't true. The biblical patriarch that comes from the early chapters in the book of Genesis represents a family that is composed of three races that are genetically related, and the family stands for a combination of many people and of many events.

Not only do the editors from the book of Genesis speak of four separate families, but they also speak of four generations, and they ascribe to each of them the name of a patriarch. Adam (the first generation) comes from the first family – Isis, Ra, El. We find an important clue in Genesis 10:1 which lists the second family from the first generation as the three sons of Noah, "Now these are the generations of the sons of Noah, Shem [the Kenizzite], Ham [the Egyptian], and Japheth [the Kenite]: and unto them were sons born after the flood." Therefore, according to the book of Genesis, the sons of Noah, who are the second family, populated the earth: they went each in different directions to their respective corners of the globe.

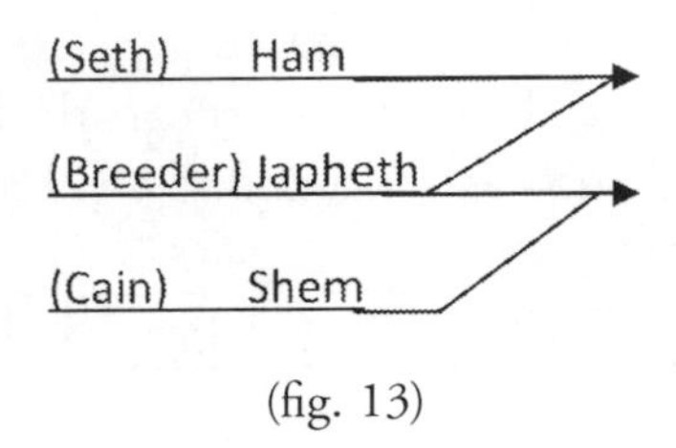

(fig. 13)

We read in Genesis 12:1, "Now the Lord said unto Abram, Get thee out of thy country, and from thy kindred, and from thy father's house, unto a land that I will shew thee." Then, in (Genesis 12:5) we read, "And Abram [the Hittite] took Sarai his wife [the Jebusite], and Lot his brother's son [the Canaanite]…and they went forth to go into the land of Canaan." Once again we are confronted with three races which comprise the third family for the third generation.

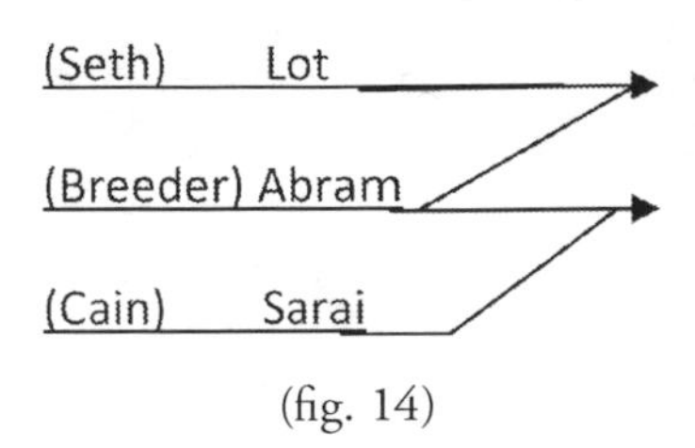

(fig. 14)

It becomes clear in Genesis 15:5 that Abram is selected to represent the third generation, "And he [the Seven Headed Serpent] brought him [Abram] forth abroad, and said, Look now toward heaven, and tell the stars, if thou be able to number them; and he said unto him, so shall thy seed [the third generation] be."

In addition, Genesis 17:7, places the fourth family – Isaac -- to the fourth generation which is represented by Abraham, "And I [the Seven Headed Serpent] will establish my covenant between me and thee [Abraham] and thy seed [the fourth family] after thee in their generation." Clearly, we have described, in the verses we have just examined, the four generations.

Well, it now becomes fundamental to pose the question: how long is a biblical generation? Genesis, chapter five, verses one to thirty-two supplies the answer. When we add the ages of the ten patriarchs since Adam, we derive at the total of 8,575 years. Then, we take this sum to divide it by the four generations to derive at the dividend of 2,143 years; therefore, it appears the biblical generation is at the minimum 2,143 years long.

NAME	AGE
Adam	930
Seth	912
Enos	905
Cainan	910
Mahalaleel	895
Jared	962
Enoch	365
Methuselah	969
Lamech	777
Noah	950
	Total = 8575

(fig. 15).

There remains the comparison for us to make to show that each generation is equal in time to the four preceding zodiac ages, and each of the 12 zodiac ages (a subject we will discuss in chapter six) is 2,160 years long. To test this hypothesis, we will multiply 2,160 to the four preceding zodiac ages in the Mayan Calendar (end Pisces, end Aires, end Taurus, end Gemini) to derive at the time factor which represents 8,640 years ago, so the generation of Adam ended around (8640 – 2011=) 6629 B.C. at the end to the Age of Gemini.

The Five Mayan Ages and the Five Generations

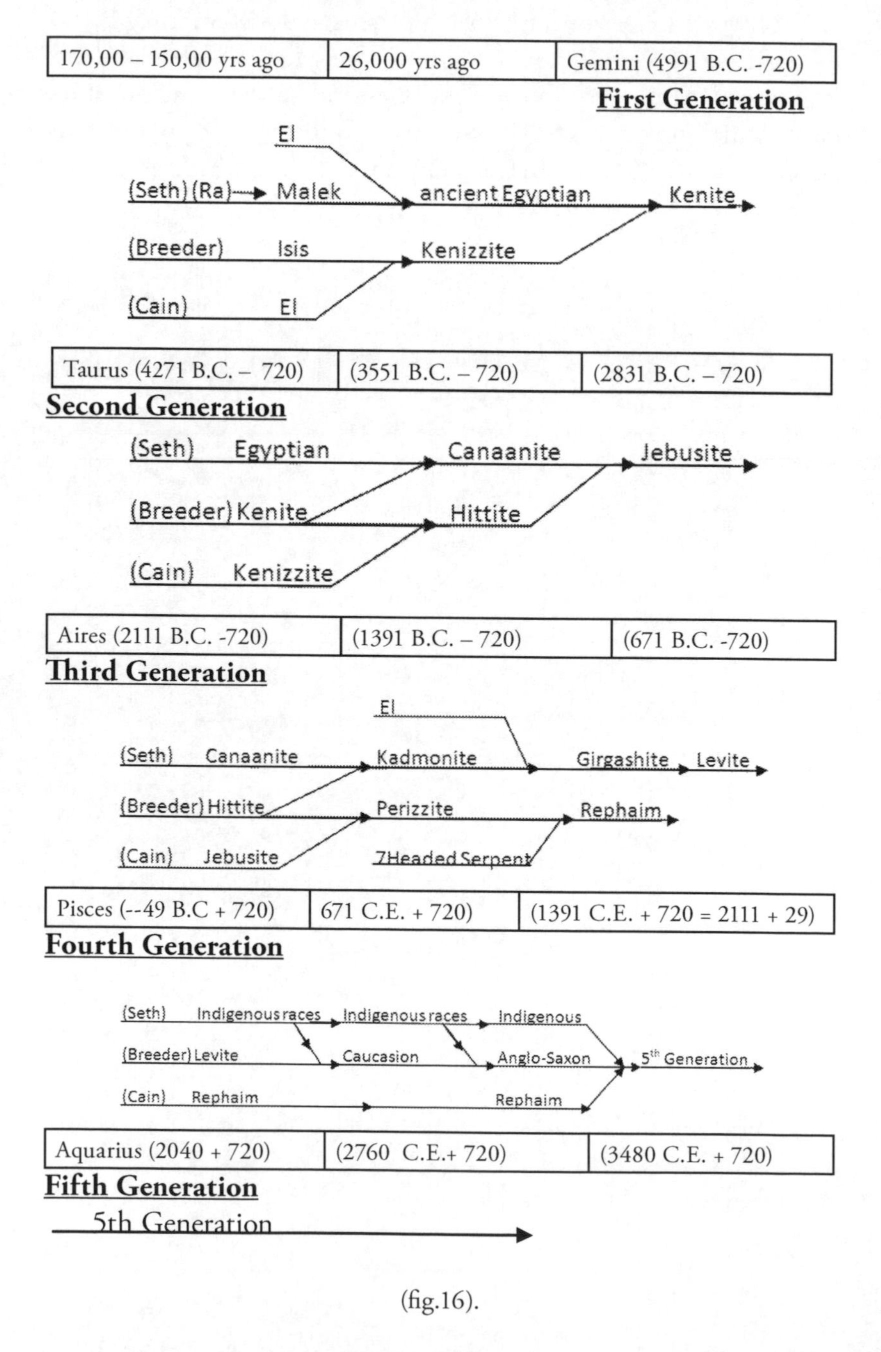

(fig.16).

When 8,575 (the biblical sum in years for the four generations) is subtracted from 8,640 (the sum in zodiac years for the four previous ages), we are left with the difference of 65 years. This amount, in the total number of years of the four generations, approximates to be incredibly accurate to the 8,640 years that is required for the four previous ages to occur.

Furthermore, we calculated earlier that a biblical generation is to be at the minimum 2,143 years long which also computes closely (with the difference of only 17 years) to the 2,160 years that are needed for the zodiac age to occur. If this reasoning is still insufficient to justify the argument that the four generations are equal in time to the zodiac ages, we will consider the following: the sign of the zodiac for the Age of Gemini (two twins) becomes highlighted in the book of Genesis through the story of Esau and Jacob who were themselves fraternal twins. Likewise, in the book of Exodus, which occurs during the Age of Taurus (the Bull), the Israelites transgress against Yahweh's commandments when they begin to idolize and to worship in place of Yahweh, the golden bull. Also, the sign for the Age of Aires (the Ram) becomes characterized in the Bible through the symbol and the sound made from the ram's horn, and the sign for this Common Era, which has become so symbolic of Jesus, represents the present Age of Pisces (the fish).

Although the Old Testament is to go through a period of editing that will span some 800 years, the different editors (known as the E,J,D, and P-schools) were careful to maintain the integrity in the total amount in years of the four generations. A total of 1,142 years are added to the generations of Adam (Genesis 5:1-32) to compensate for the editing; the solar calendar became implemented approximately 3,150 years ago and marked that moment in time when the first edit was introduced, and by doing so, it mysteriously reveals the age of the flood.

We read in Genesis 5: 23-24, "And all the days of Enoch were three hundred sixty and five years [a solar year]: And Enoch walked with God: and he was not; for God took him." Enoch departed from earth when he was 365 years old –the precise length in days of the solar year. We continue with Genesis 5:28-31, "And Lamech lived an hundred eighty and two years, and begat a son: And he called his name Noah… And all the days of Lamech were seven hundred seventy and seven years: and he died."

Once again we find a significant pattern in a patriarch's age, for it is not a coincidence that Lamech, the father of Noah, dies exactly at the age of 777 years. No! This isn't to be! Surely, this isn't the case at all: the three sevens that are reflected in Lamech's age signify the biblical flood. The first seven stands for the seven days in advance warning the Seven Headed Serpent gave to Noah; the second seven represents the seven days that elapsed since the first dove was sent to find land, and the third seven signifies the seven days that elapsed since the second dove didn't return back to the ark. When the ages of Enoch and Lamech are added together, we derive at the sum of 1,142 years, and if we add 1,142 to 8,225 (the age of the ten patriarchs before the flood which is determined by subtracting 350 from Noah's age), we derive at the number that represents 9,367 years ago; thus, the biblical flood ended (9367-2011) around 7356 B.C.

According to the Bible, the second family emerged when Noah was 500 years old (8,575-500+1,142 = 9,217 years ago), and it ended 450 years later (9,217-450 = 8,767 years) in 6756 B.C. when Noah died at the age of nine hundred and fifty years. The second generation which is called Noah began when the first generation which is called Adam blended into the second family near the end of the Age of Gemini 600 years before the biblical flood (9,967 years ago). The third generation which is called Abram climaxed roughly 2,500 years ago at the end to the Age of Aires, for a time it co-existed with the fourth family before blending into the fourth generation which is called Abraham some 2,100 years ago at the dawn to the present Age of Pisces.

According to the mandate from the seven heavens, genes from the life-form with a spirit of consciousness (Malek) that had the spirit of the angel Michael imparted into it and genes from the Son of God that had been imparted with the Elohim spirit were to be implanted separately inside the womb of feminine Malek to procreate alien life on the earth some one hundred seventy thousand years ago. But the creation of alien life never occurred! By mating Isis with the Sons of God, an Agenda interrupted the creation of alien life on the earth. One hundred seventy-one thousand years later, on the second visit to earth (roughly 9,000 years ago), Isis used her womb to create the line of Cain, and then, an Agenda used the womb of feminine Malek to create the line of Seth.

Now, To create the Huzin-man race an Agenda first genetically combined genes from masculine Malek with genes from a female Kenizzite to procreate the ancient Egyptian (Seth) within the womb of Malek; then, it genetically combined genes of the ancient Egyptian female with genes from the male Kenizzite (Cain) to create the Kenite (Enos) within the womb of the ancient Egyptian. The Kenite took 130 years (Adam's age before Seth is born) to emerge. Adam's life-span of 930 years indicates the length in time that it takes for the genes of Malek to blend and to fade into the genes of the ancient Egyptian people. Nine hundred and twelve years later (Seth's life-span) the Kenite people blend into the Canaanite race, and it takes another 905 years (Enos' life-span) for the Canaanite race to blend into the genes called the Kadmonite race.

When we examine the ages of Adam, Seth, Enos (930, 912, 905.), we discern a descending pattern in the number of years that corresponds directly to their ages, but these numbers do not represent the patriarchs' life-span; instead, they represent the ages of the races that come from the line of Seth that have each assimilated themselves into the subsequent generation. Therefore, the approximate number of 900 years represents the assimilation period. By the time the generation of Abram arrived, the assimilation period had shortened to approximate 600 years

	Breeding period	Assimilation period
Seth	800	930 (Adam's age)
Enos	807	912 (Seth's age)
Cainan	815	905 (Enos'es) age)
Mahalaleel	840	910 (Cainan's age)
Total	3262	3657

(fig. 17).

The most important concept to remember about the assimilation period is that it de-generates the human spirit for the following generation. In the bible, degeneration is referred to as transgression, and transgression of the human spirit in the human brain was necessary for the human conscious to develop.

Hence, the human race was transgressed for approximately 2,300 years. First, the 2nd generation was transgressed unwillingly for the last 800 years before assimilating into the third family when man's Michael spirit degraded to the required level that allows for consciousness to develop; then, an Agenda put to breed the third generation for over 1,500 years before the human being with the propensity for the conscious emerged.

Thus, by 500 B.C. near the end of the Age of Aires, the story of the human race and the subsequent development of the human conscious begins (Genesis 15:12-13), "...As the sun was going down, a deep sleep fell upon Abram; and, lo, a horror of great darkness fell upon him. And he [the Seven Headed Serpent] said unto Abram…. But in the fourth generation they [the angels Michael, Ra, and Viracocha] shall come hither again; for the iniquity [the transgression] of the Amorites [of man's Michael spirit] is not yet full." Cloudy, ambiguous, the truth behind the verses true meaning remains unknown, yet the biblical Lord does warn Abram about the coming of the fourth generation when the angels will come to thwart an Agenda's scheme to prevent the creation of the Rephaim people.

Hidden within the biblical story is the fact that Abram is a Hittite and Sarai is a Jebusite, and they fulfilled an unknown covenant for the biblical Lord by procreating an interracial child from the Line of Cain -- the supposed progenitor to the human conscious that came from the Perizzite race better known to us as the tribe of Benjamin. An Agenda chose males from the tribe of Benjamin to donate their genes to create the Rephaim people, but now it didn't require the mating ritual. Absolutely not! Now, it required the scientific manipulation of alien and human genes. Genes from the male Perizzite were combined with spirit from the Seven Headed Serpent, and the mixture was implanted inside the womb of the female Perizzite. Nine months later – the Rephaim (Chinese people) were born

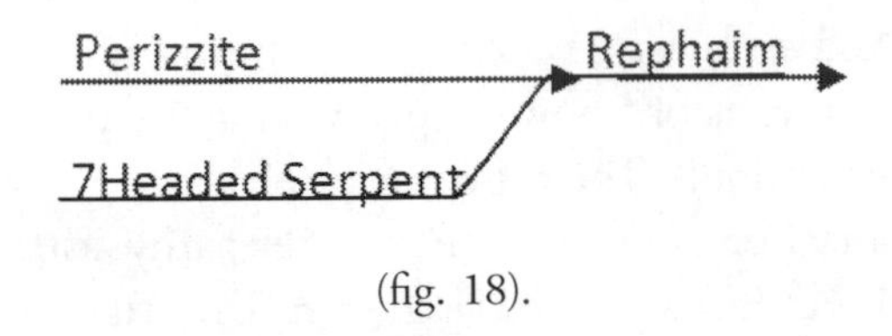

(fig. 18).

Abram and Sarai fulfilled the unknown covenant, but the scientifically genetically manipulated Rephaim people did not develop a conscious, and nowhere else could this unknown mystery become clearer than through the writings of the Mayan (Kenite) culture whose people were the half-descendants to both the line of Cain and the line of Seth. In the Mayan *Popul Voh* by Dennis Tedlock, Part Four page 165 which is entitled *here is the beginning of the conception of humans* we read, "These were the... first people [Rephaim] who were made and modeled... They talked and they made words. They looked and they listened. They walked, they worked...Thoughts came into existence and they gazed; their vision came all at once. Perfectly they saw, perfectly they knew everything under the sky, whenever they looked. The moment they turned around and looked around in the sky, on the earth, everything was seen without any obstruction. They didn't have to walk around before they could see what was under the sky; they just stayed where they were. As they looked, their knowledge became intense. Their sight passed through trees, through rocks, through lakes, through seas, through mountains, through plains."

There remains the curious connection that exists between the story in the Garden of Eden (when man and woman are banished from the Garden to prevent them from eating from the tree of life) and the story in the Popul Vuh (when the makers, the begetters are displeased with the creation of the superiorly advanced Rephaim people). The gods in the Popul Vuh echoed the story in the Garden of Eden when they took away the newly created Rephaim people's superior understanding.

They (page 167), "...changed the nature of their works, their designs, it was enough that the eyes be marred by the Heart of Sky. They were blinded as the face of a mirror is breathed upon. Their eyes were weakened. Now it was only when they looked nearby things were clear. And such was the loss of the means of understanding, along with the means of knowing everything, by the four humans [the fourth generation]. The root was implanted."

Clairvoyance, precognition, mental telepathy, astral projection and other forms of ESP – those are the remnants that man's Michael spirit has left behind. Yet the Michael spirit was still so much greater than the forces man calls ESP, and it was this level in the Michael spirit of a Perizzite that prevented Abram and Sarai from fulfilling the unknown covenant.

Now, it was through the genes of Neanderthal that an Agenda brought forth consciousness to the human race. Because Sarai came from the line of Cain, she possessed a maximum five percent of Neanderthal in her genes, but Hagar, who came from the line of Seth, possessed a maximum ten percent. Because of this, an Agenda focused on Hagar, Abram's maid.

When the Seven Headed Serpent entered into the known biblical covenant with Abram, it was to produce a male offspring from a female who came from the line of Seth, so Abram did so without Sarai. Therefore, he followed the directions to fulfill the covenant by having sexual intercourse with his "Canaanite" not his Egyptian maid Hagar, and she conceived him a son. Thus, the story of

Ishmael becomes synonymous with Sarai's barrenness and becomes the key to unlock the mystery behind the first biblical covenant.

Yes it is true! Sarai's biblical sterility excluded her from the covenant, but it is untrue that she was infertile, for that supposed infertility explains why Ishmael brought forth consciousness yet didn't inherit the human conscious. Ishmael was an interracial child that came from Abram and Hagar. Because of the lineage to his father Abram, Ishmael came from the line of Cain. Although the line of Cain brought forth consciousness through the Afro-Asiatic races, it didn't develop the human conscious because Ishmael (the ten tribes of Israel) came from a father who comes from the line of Cain. Therefore, the biblical Lord created another covenant, but this time it is with Abraham to bring forth a male from the tribe of Judah whose father comes from the line of Seth.

To create the human conscious, an Agenda had to first develop consciousness in the brain. To accomplish this goal, an Agenda devised a scheme that would create a half sister for Abraham. We read in Genesis 16:4, "And he [Abram] went in unto Hagar, and she conceived…" Hagar conceived Ishmael because Sarai was biblically barren, or was she. Maybe her barrenness didn't mean she can't conceive an offspring for Abram. Perhaps it meant Sarai couldn't produce an Afro-Asiatic male heir because she came from the line of Cain. Since Sarai was a Jebusite and Abram was a Hittite, they couldn't produce a male heir that came from the line of Seth,

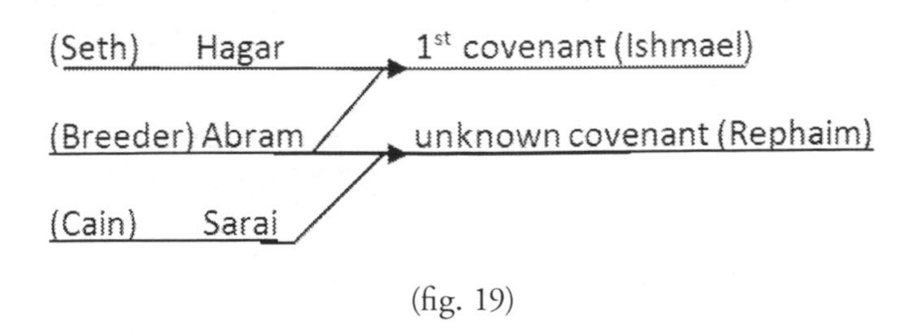

(fig. 19)

but the second covenant specifically required an interracial offspring to come from the line of Seth.

On the flip side, Hagar was a Canaanite and Abram was a Hittite, and together they produced a male heir for the line of Seth: Ishmael. The covenant has been revealed! By requirement, the male heir to the Afro-Asiatic races came from the half-sister to Abram, and the half-sister was to come from the line of Seth. Although Sarai was a half-sister to Abram, she came from the line of Cain, so she could never produce an interracial child to meet an Agenda's covenant.

Now, what does this, technical, half-sister mumbo-jumble jargon really mean? Well, the important clue comes in knowing that Sarai was a Jebusite from the line of Cain and Sarah was a Kadmonite from the line of Seth, so they were half-sisters through their racial not through their parental lineage. Sarai fulfilled the unknown covenant from the line of Cain – the creation of the Chinese people. Hagar fulfilled the known covenant from the line of Seth – the creation of the Kadmonite race. Hagar was a half-sister to Sarah and to Abram, so an Agenda focused on her because she came from the line of Seth (a mixture of ancient Egyptian and Kenizzite); however, because of the Kenizzite connection (a mixture of El and Isis), an Agenda had to breed the line of Seth with the line of Cain.

Ishmael was chosen to pave the way for the arrival to the human conscious by bringing consciousness through the twelve tribes of Israel (the Kadmonite races). He emerged during a time when the second (with the exception of the Kenite people) and the third generation plus the Amorite no longer walked on the earth. They existed in man within the different percentages of genes that are found within the Afro-Asiatic races. Verses 18 and 19 from Genesis chapter 15 make this fact dubiously clear, "In the same day the Lord made a covenant with Abram, saying, unto thy seed [Ishmael] have I given this land, from the river of Egypt [Africa] unto the great river, the river Euphrates [Asia]. The Kenites [Mayan people], and the Kenizzites [ancient Oriental people], and the Kadmonites [Afro-Asiatic races]. And the Hittites [Oriental race], and the Perizzites [Chinese race], and the Rephaims [Chinese people]. And the Amorites [Malek], and the Canaanites [African race], and the Girgashites [future Levite people], and the Jebusites [Asian race]."

But if Ishmael inherited the genes from the second and the third generations, who would inherit the genes from the fourth? Well -- Abraham's covenant with God entails itself around his son Isaac (Genesis 17:1), "And when Abram was ninety years old and nine, the Lord appeared to Abram, and said unto him, I am the almighty God; walk before me, and be thou perfect."

Introduced at the tender age of ninety-nine, Abram enters into another covenant with the biblical Lord (Genesis 17:2), "And I will make my covenant between me and thee, and will multiply thy seed [Isaac] exceedingly." But there comes an unexpected twist in the turn of events as Genesis 17:5 shifts away the importance from the name Abram and places it toward the name of Abraham, "Neither shall thy name any more be called Abram [a Hittite name], but thy name shall be Abraham [a Kadmonite name]."

Thus, the biblical verses delineated the moment an Agenda shifted the importance away from the line of Cain and toward the line of Seth in order to create Isaac. In an earlier verse (Genesis 16:16), we learn, "...Abram was fourscore and six years old, when Hagar bore Ishmael to Abram." If we do the math (99-86 = 13), we will find a 13 year difference between the ages not only of Ishmael and Isaac but also of Abram and Abraham.

Modern consensus holds steadfast to the opinion that Abram and Abraham are the same person and that Abram was 99 when he changed his name to Abraham. For what reason did the biblical Lord instruct Abram to change his name? Was it because he left Ur and relocated with his family to Canaan? Isn't it true that Abram originated from Ur but Abraham didn't? So doesn't this mean they were two different people and not one person with two different personality-traits?

Because of the vagueness, the obscurity, we will reveal in the following verses, we concluded that Abram and Abraham were half-brothers who came from two distinct but related races and that they came from the third family which belonged to the third generation. Although these statements may appear as mere speculation, this is precisely the case.

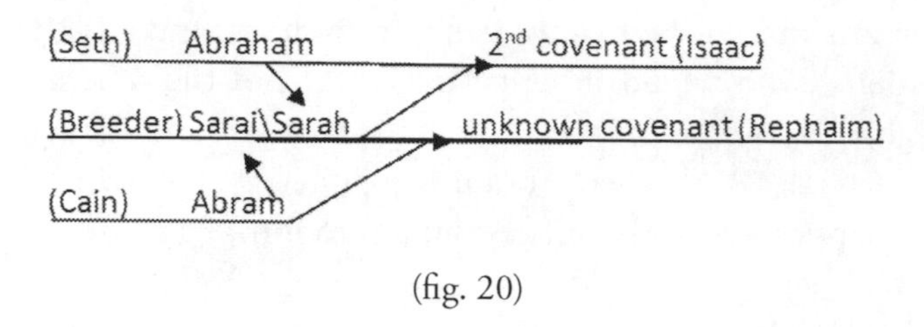

(fig. 20)

According to Genesis 17: 5, Abram changed his name when he entered into another covenant with the biblical Lord. Suddenly! The name of Abram and of Sarai no longer matters! Now, the name of Abraham and Sarah did, and Sarah was to bring forth the progenitor to the human conscious. When the two stories are compared, they show two inconsistencies that point toward the fact that Abram and Abraham were two different persons.

First, whenever Abram encounters the Lord, the biblical verses make no mention that he would fall on his face. For example, we read in Genesis 15:1, "After these things the word of the Lord came unto Abram in a vision, saying, Fear not, Abram: I am thy shield, and thy exceeding great reward. And Abram said, Lord God…" We find no mention that he fell on his face, but immediately after Abram enters into the second covenant and changes his name to Abraham we read (Genesis 17:2-3), "And I will make my covenant between me and thee, and will multiply thee exceedingly. And Abram fell on his face: and God talked with him."

Apparently, it appears, since the moment Abram changed his name to Abraham, he immediately but curiously began to fall on his face whenever he encountered the biblical Lord, but to fall on one's face became a custom that is incurred by the line of Seth not by the line of Cain. Today in modern Jerusalem, as well as in other parts of the world, a person squats down and bends forward to touch the forehead to the ground as a sign of respect in reverence to God.

Secondly, the name Abram is rooted within the line of Cain because it originates from the Hittite race, and the name Abraham is rooted within the line of Seth because it originates from the ancient Egyptian people. Abram was 86 years old when Abraham was ninety-nine. There is a difference of thirteen years that exists between them. This difference marks the time when the Afro-Asiatic races (the 12 tribes of Israel) acquired consciousness. This time highlights the moment when the first male and female Ishmaelites became thirteen years old and could begin to reproduce.

Ishmael was thirteen when Isaac was born, and both of them came from the Twelve Tribes of Israel, and according to the second covenant, a tribe that came from the Afro-Asiatic races would inherit the human conscious. Is it possible that the story of Isaac is the story of two tribes of people that separated from the Twelve Tribes of Israel? One tribe (Benjamin -- the descendants of the Rephaim people) came from the line of Cain and could not fulfill the first covenant. The other (Judah – the descendants of the Girgashite people), came from the line of Seth and would fulfill the second covenant. The remaining ten tribes became the descendants of the Arab nations, and they were chosen to fulfill the first covenant.

We will examine the past, just after the biblical flood, to understand a 2,400 year-old controversy and learn how it developed (Genesis 9:20-22), "And Noah began to be a husband man, and he planted a vineyard: And he drank of the wine, and was drunken; and he was uncovered within his tent. And Ham [an Egyptian], the father of Canaan [an African], saw the nakedness [the mating ritual] of his father, and told his two brethren without."

These verses carry within them a secret meaning that conveys the Egyptian people became aware of an Agenda's transgression of the line of Seth, and they tried to warn the Kenite and the Kenizzite people. Instead, a chastisement and a condemnation followed Ham's offspring -- the African race. Genesis chapter nine, verses twenty-four to twenty-five, "And Noah awoke from his wine, and knew what his younger son [Ham] had done unto him [revealed his involvement in the mating ritual]. And he said, Cursed be Canaan [the African race]; a servant of servants [a slave] shall he be unto his brethren."

Thus, an Agenda enslaved the Canaanite race which belongs to the line of Seth and forced them to practice the mating ritual. Not only did this curse associate the African race with the insult of slavery, but also, it created the twelve tribes of Israel, and as we have just learned, the twelve tribes became man's precursor to the human conscious.

Discovered with the Dead Sea Scrolls, in the Cave of Qumran, along with the book of Enoch, is a work entitled *Prologue on the Sons of Jared* which contains an account of the final degeneration of the line of Seth through its participation in the mating ritual. In the same manner Malek was protected in a dwelling atop an impenetrable summit, so were (according to the *Prologue to the Sons of Jared*) the last descendants from the line of Seth protected atop an impenetrable summit within the Cave of Treasures. We begin with (chapter 19:4-5) as God commands Jared to not, "... go thou again out of the cave, until thou receivest an order through a vision, and not in an apparition, when seen by thee. Then, command again thy people not to hold intercourse with the children [line] of Cain, and not to learn their ways."

Evidently, the Lord (in this case the angel Michael) instructed Jared not to be deceived by an apparition (by his eyes), but to wait until he is contacted through a vision (through his mind) before he goes outside of the cave, and the Lord also instructed Jared to warn the line of Seth to stay inside the Cave of Treasures so as not to fall prey to the mating ritual with the line of Cain. The story began with Genun who was responsible for conducting the mating ritual. Satan taught him how to play beautiful music to touch one's heart and how to ferment a strong alcoholic beverage out of corn. Genun combined his music and his drinks to corrupt the line of Cain. Soon, sin multiplied and drunkenness and hatred and murder increased within the children of Cain.

Now, we continue (Prologue 20:11-12), "Genun gathered together companies upon companies, that played on horns..., at the foot of the Holy Mountain; and they did so in order that the children of Seth who were on the Holy Mountain should hear it. But when the children of Seth heard the noise, they wondered, and came by companies, and stood on top of the mountain to look at those below; and they did thus a whole year."

The verses make it clear. The mating ritual occurred in great numbers and was accompanied by alcoholic intoxication; it was the same intoxication that Noah had succumbed to immediately after the flood. Again, Satan interjected to teach Genun to make beautifying dyes, and now the children of Cain shone in beauty and gorgeous attire, and they (Prologue 20:14), "...gathered together at the foot of the mountain in splendour, with horns and gorgeous dresses, and horse races, committing all manner of abominations."

Little by little, the children of Seth were being won over to the mating ritual. Finally, one day (Prologue 20:17-18) the, "... children of Cain looked up from below, and saw the children of Seth, standing in troops on the top of the mountain; and they called to them to come down to them. But the children of Seth said to them from above, "We don't know the way."

Immediately, Satan intervened to instruct Genun to tell the children of Seth how they could descend from the mountain. Despite Jared's wise council to not go down, they descended from the holy mountain (Prologue 20:31-33), "And when they looked at the daughters of Cain, at their beautiful figures, and at their hands and feet dyed with colour, and tattooed in ornaments on their faces, the fire of sin was kindled in them. Then Satan made them look most beautiful before the sons of Seth, as he also made the sons of Seth appear of the fairest in the eyes of the daughters of Cain, so that the daughters of Cain lusted after the sons of Seth like ravenous beasts, and the sons of Seth after the daughters of Cain, until they committed abomination with them. But after they had thus fallen into this defilement, they returned by way they had come, and tried to ascend the Holy Mountain. But they could not, because the stones of that Holy Mountain were of fire flashing before them."

Company by company, the children of Seth continued to descend from the mountain until just Methuselah, Lamech, and Noah remained. The direct descendants to the second family of the human race called the Huzin-people had succumbed to the mating ritual. Certainly, the religious and political ramifications the ancient mating ritual has effected upon the cultures of the middle-East have not gone unnoticed.

In the 21st century there developed a 2,400 year-old controversy between two cultures of people both claiming to be the rightful heirs to the promise land -- the perceived descendants to Ishmael (the Palestinian state) or the perceived descendants to Isaac (the Jewish state).

To put religious fervor and political asylum aside, the controversy has divided nations, peoples, and beliefs while up-rooting wars, conflicts, and debates. Yet it is an established fact that Islam derived from Ishmael and that Hebrew as a religion derived from Isaac, and both of them have been in constant conflict from the start. To this end, we will explain what the covenant for Ishmael and the covenant for Isaac truly means, for both of the covenants go woven together hand by hand to show that Ishmael had to fulfill the first covenant before Isaac was ever born because consciousness through the Ismaelite called Sarah brought forth the human conscious through the Girgashite called Isaac.

As we understand, an Agenda didn't choose Isaac over Ishmael because it equally needed from the both of them, and the promise-land that they were going to inherit was a breeding laboratory in Canaan. Ishmael inherited not a land but consciousness; Isaac inherited the human conscious. Man has yet to understand the simple yet over-looked fact that Ishmael and Isaac as well as Abram and Abraham and the other patriarchs that come before them were not individual persons but individual races. Ishmael represents the Afro-Asiatic races, and they introduced consciousness to the fourth generation; Isaac represents the Girgashite people, and they introduced the human conscious to the fourth generation. Sarai represents the Rephaim people, and they were originally expected to inherit the human conscious.

Therefore, we have uncovered the untenable, the unpalatable, the unacceptable, reality: the biblical covenant came from an Agenda that belongs to a Snake. Abram was a Hittite that originated from Ur from the land of Sumer which was under the control of Isis. On the other hand, Abraham was a Canaanite that originated from the land of Canaan which was under the control of El, and the Seven

Headed Serpent (Satan) would later control an Agenda of a Snake on the earth.

Ishmael came to represent the ten tribes of Israel; Isaac came to represent the group of Afro-Asiatic people from the tribe of Judah who were chosen to fulfill the second covenant; the tribe of Benjamin came to represent the unknown covenant whose purpose it was to create the Rephaim people. Will man ever come to understand the truth! There is to be no honor, no prestige, no gratification, for the descendants of Ishmael, Isaac, the Rephaim people, to know the human being is the result of the contrived and deliberate creation of a people that would serve a mysterious and unknown agenda for a group of disobedient angels who fell from the will and the benevolence of the true God of the Universe. Plainly! The Ishmaelite couldn't inherit the human conscious because the Ishmaelite fathered Isaac – the Girgashite people!

Therefore, by the end of the Age of Aires (about 120 B.C.) man was transgressed to the level that allowed for the human brain to develop the human conscious. After the Afro-Asiatic races developed consciousness, an Agenda was aware it would require, one final act, one final expose, to create the human conscious, and once more it wasn't going to involve itself around the mating ritual. No! This time it required the scientific manipulation of alien and human genes.

In the second biblical story of creation, before the man and the woman are placed in the Garden of Eden (Genesis 2: 9), "out of the ground made the Lord God [Elohim] to grow every tree that is pleasant to the sight, and good for food; the tree of life [man's Michael spirit] also in the midst of the garden, and the tree of knowledge of good and evil [the conscious mind]." This symbolic story of creation commemorates the moment when the human conscious was born. Because man chose to eat from the tree of knowledge, the biblical story delineates the moment when man lost contact with his Michael spirit (because he ate from the tree of knowledge of good and evil and not from the tree of life) and enters into the world of the conscious mind.

Thirteen years after the Kadmonite races developed consciousness the Girgashite people were created, and they came from the spirit of El and from genes of the male from the tribe of Judah.

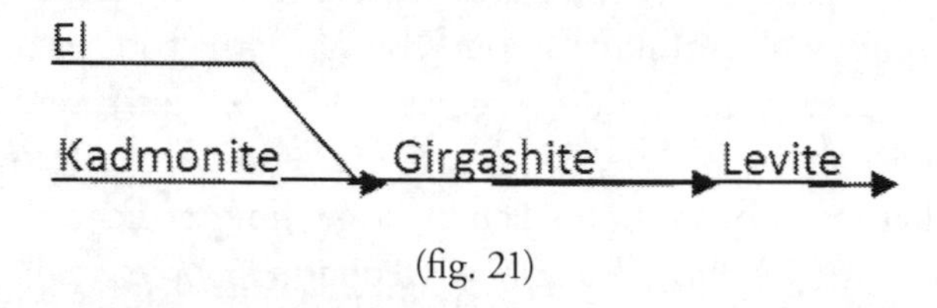

(fig. 21)

The mixture became implanted into the wombs of female Ishmaelites. Nine months later the Girgashite was born. The male measured about six feet and weighed approximately 200 pounds. The Girgashite had straight blonde hair and a white colored complexion. Originally, the Girgashite people were born with the propensity to develop the human conscious, so an Agenda conditioned them for some 50 years before the male Girgashite with the human conscious emerged; thus, by 120 B.C., at the end to the Age of Aires, the beginning of the human race and the newly developed human conscious begins

CHAPTER FIVE

Entrapment of Man's Michael Spirit

To construct the framework from which to explain man's entrapped human spirit, we will embark on the search for evidence that takes us well into the realms of the hypothetical possibility. We will compare the human race to a group of captured mice. They are scurrying about in a cage. The mice have become the unwilling participants to an experiment that is being performed by the human scientist -- an incomprehensible intelligence when compared to the inconsequential awareness of the captured mice. The mice dart about and around in the cage in every conceivable direction. Disoriented, confused, unfamiliar with the surroundings -- they have entered into a state of total frenzy.

The mice learn to accomplish tasks that are set for them by the human and learn how to differentiate between them. Soon they discover if they press a certain color lever it brings them food and water, but if they press the wrong color, pain will result. With time, the mice learn to differentiate between the two colors, so they continue to be rewarded over and over again. When their responses become instinctive and automatic and continue even when food and water isn't available, the mice have become conditioned and will continue to repeat a response for as long as the scientist continues to sporadically repeat a reward.

Our attention now focuses away from the mice that are inside the cage to the far reaches of the Caucasoid mountains; from there, we will compare the mice's unfortunate predicament to the forgotten calamity of the Girgashite people. They live within the Caucasoid Mountains sequestered inside the protected sector which is controlled by an Agenda of a Snake – an omnipotent intelligence when compared to the inconsequential awareness of the newly created Girgashite people. They walk about and around the sector seemingly in super- slow motion. Disoriented, confused, unfamiliar with the surrounding terrain, the newly created human people have entered into a state of complete and total shock.

Girgashite people learn to accomplish tasks that are set for them by an Agenda. They learn how to follow rules and how to submit to regulations. Through these ordinances, the humans learn to work for the expenditure of money. They learn to visit the temple to serve the omnipotent God. They learn to condition their families to do the same. By following rules, the Girgashite people are rewarded with food, water, and basic necessities. When their responses become instinctive and automatic and continue even when necessities aren't available, the Girgashite people have become conditioned and will continue to repeat the response for as long as an Agenda continues to sporadically repeat the reward.

Does this imaginary scenario explain the precarious predicament of the human race? We contend that it does, and we believe there is an internal factor within man's mind that he has yet to become aware of that seems to be unconsciously dictating his life through the selfish use of money and through the false adoration of earthly gods. The Mayan civilization had no concept for the word money. The Mayan people (like the Indigenous cultures that followed) were rich in gold which adorned them and their temples. Their temples were aligned to the celestial positions of the earth and sky. Despite the negative connotations that have been attributed to the Maya, they did not practice human sacrifice and were not a war-like people.

The idea the Mayans practiced human sacrifice derives from the interpretation of the Mayan script. We contend it is impossible for anyone to interpret Mayan script because it (like the Sumerian Cuneiform and the Egyptian hieroglyphic writing) is the art of communicating through mental telepathy. Any attempt that someone takes to interpret this symbolical story language of the mind through the alphabetical written language of man will be subject for error.

How could a people that were free from the constraints of money, that were free from the plague of disease, that have bequeathed to man a calendar that foretells his future, practice human sacrifice.

The idea is foolish. Untrue! Now, it is true that sometime after the Mayan culture disappeared and the Spaniards invaded the New World the human race as a whole has become conditioned to use money.

There remains the question to ponder as to why man uses money. The worn out excuse that it replaced the barter system is simply not going to be enough. If money is meant to benefit society, why does the majority of people have so little of it and why do so few people have so much. Generally speaking, can it be a coincidence that money is so disproportionately spread throughout the different ethnic groups.

The Anglo-Saxon races brought the concept of money to the New World and by doing so broke the natural state of equilibrium that was being maintained by the Native American people for the animals. Money derived from the Catholic Church. Written on any U.S. currency are the words in God we trust. This means that in the beginning religion and government were two factions acting as one entity. Today religion and government have become separate and opposing factions, but this was not the case when an Agenda of a Snake was conditioning the Girgashite people.

Therefore, we will conclude that a thought process that originated from a group of fallen angels preceded the social structure of the human race. Furthermore, in human society man's physical laws and regulations originate from an alien blueprint that is intended to condition a chosen Girgashite people to develop a conscious mind all the while living within a specific government created by an Agenda of a Snake.

We begin with the story of the Levite people in Minoa Crete around 500 B.C. where the Levite army was spreading an Agenda of a Snake and established the first humanly operated government by the Aegean Sea thereby enslaving the indigenous Minoan population. First, the Levite army slowly spread into Greece and into Rome; then, it dispersed throughout the continent of Europe and established a hierarchy of governments that further enslaved the indigenous populations in those regions. By A.D. 500, a centralized government became established through an Agenda called the

Catholic Reformation. First, it established a system of Christian governments throughout Europe that spread itself throughout the free world. From Europe, an Agenda spread into North and South Africa, and into the Arab nations, and into the Caribbean and Central and South and North America to reach the outer most corners of the globe.

Anglo-land is the previous name of England because it represents a home for the Anglo-Saxon. As a descendant of the Caucasian, the Anglo-Saxon spread the same ideology, and the Caucasian spread the same agenda of the Levite people, and they spread an Agenda of a Snake. Also, there remains a virtually unknown yet curious fact about the name government, for it derives from the composite of two Latin words – In Spanish government means governar (to control) mente (the mind); thus, according to the literal Spanish translation, the true purpose for government is to control a peoples mind.

Furthermore, the idea to enslave then to later control a human people didn't originate from a human mind. Of course not! How could it! The human mind was unable to create the idea to govern in the first place. Didn't you know the Girgashite people were in an experimental stage when an Agenda imposed itself at full force! An answer means only one sure thing. An alien Agenda created the idea over 2,500 years ago, and as we compare the human conscious to the mind of the mice in our story, we will discover the human conscious resulted from a deliberate experiment that, in the final outcome, turned out terribly wrong. In the case for the Girgashite people, the experiment was designed to create a propensity to acquire the highly awaited conscious mind. For the fallen angels, the experiment turned out to be a complete and absolute disaster.

Therefore, with the appearance of the conscious mind, man signified a time when he began to think carnally as opposed to immaterially, when he began to behave emotionally as opposed to spiritually. During the second generation, the second family lived by the will of the Michael and Huzin spirits, so they had mastered physical limitations. Sleep, food, and water presented no stumbling blocks for them.

However, by the end of the first-half to the Age of Taurus, the line of Cain (the Kenizzite people) began to live by the will of an Agenda of a Snake, and they were subjected to physical limitations, so the change from immaterialism to materialism (by breeding the line of Cain with the line of Seth) occurred gradually. Some 7,000 years ago, in the first halve of the second generation, man got the closest he could ever get to the Progenitor of the Universe. Genesis chapter 6:9 implies that Noah was, "... a just man, perfect in his generations. Noah [the second generation] walked with God." At the start to the Age of Taurus, the second family had a 75% human spirit to a 25% consciousness ratio. This meant they stood perfect among the generations that followed.

Thus, the conditioning process enforced against the second family that degenerated man's Michael spirit was done slowly throughout a period of 2,500 years. First, in the last 800 years to the Age of Taurus, an Agenda introduced the Kenizzite people full force into the mating ritual: an age that was consumed solely in the degeneration of their Michael spirit; then, by the start to the Age of Aires an Agenda bred the line of Seth with the line of Cain thereby bringing the human mind closer to the sexual perversions of the mating ritual and to the unquenchable desire to acquire money. By Aires end, man's Michael spirit began to wax and to wane, to become stained then polluted, stagnated by an innate compulsion to experience sexual pleasure and corrupted by the inherent need to acquire money.

Hence, man entered the age of Pisces with a Michael spirit to consciousness ratio at 50-50%: an ideal condition for the development of the conscious mind. When the third generation entered into the age of Aires, man's Michael spirit ratio was set at 75% and his consciousness was set at a low of 25; however, by mid Aires, man's Michael spirit ratio plummeted to 51%, while his consciousness rocketed to 49; as a consequence, by the end of the Age of Aires, both ratios stood at a staggering 50-50 percent.

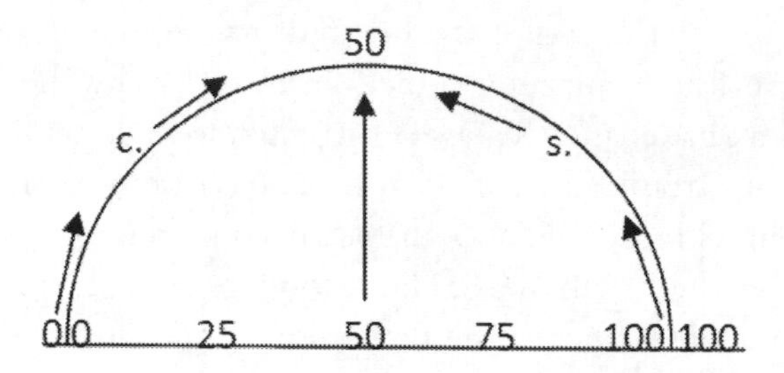

(fig. 22) Normal Michael spirit (s) to consciousness ratio (c) = 50\50%.

As a result, the human conscious entered into the age of Pisces -- lusting for sexual pleasure, guided by the will of the sexual impulse, deceived by the need to acquire money. With those factors set in motion, man's Michael spirit became impeded and began to distance itself slowly away from the anatomical area where it once resided within the human brain. By 500 B.C., the human conscious emerged and created an ongoing struggle within the mind of man: The spiritual battle between God (the human conscience) and Satan (the conscious mind).

Within the human mind, those two opposing forces manifest independent of themselves although they co-exist dependent within the genes of every human being. After the conception of the human fetus, the two forces part direction to seat themselves within the human brain. The spiritual forces of God are located within the right hemisphere, and the spiritual forces of Satan are within the left.

For the human conscious to develop, an Agenda created another hemisphere for the brain; thus, the left hemisphere appeared about 26,000 years ago with the emergence of the ancient Egyptian people. About 8,500 years ago, in the age of Taurus, the left hemisphere began to function gradually. Consciousness emerged when the left hemisphere began to function at the mid-way point and reached full maturity about 500 B.C. near an end to the Age of Aires.

The frontal lobe of the left hemisphere became the seat of man's awareness -- the area where conscious thought first developed. With time the frontal lobe of the left hemisphere obligated the frontal lobe of the right, to produce an area in the brain stem to handle the influx of incoming signals; thus, the brain stem became the seat of conscious thought and the left frontal lobe became the seat of conscious memory.

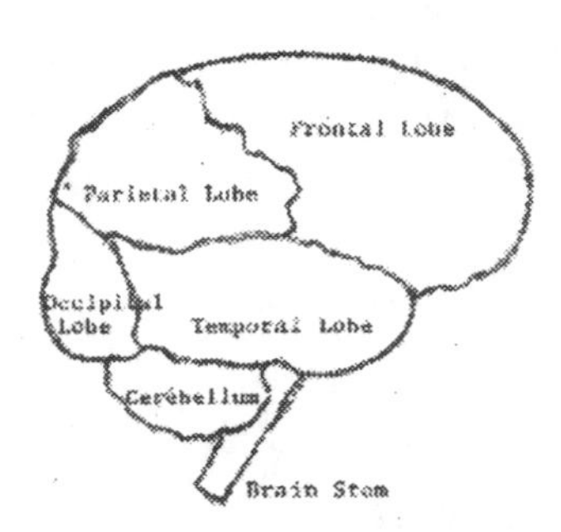

(fig. 23) Right hemisphere and brain stem.

Incoming signals consisted of sexual and instinctual stimuli. With time the conscious response to the sexual stimuli ran out of control. It is clear now! The male Levite genetically inherited a trait to satisfy his sexual impulses by engaging in group-sex – a remnant of the mating ritual he inherited from Isis, and he also inherited a trait from El – a desire to engage in sexual intercourse for pleasure. Combined together, those two genetic traits created a recipe for disaster for the fallen angels.

Have you figured it out! In order to free El and Isis from their confinements on earth's 14th and 15th dimensions, the Seven Headed Serpent created the Girgashite people. In those dimensions, each individual El spirit and each individual Isis spirit lived in a state of solitary confinement, so when the moment for them to escape was un-veiled, they immediately and knowingly trapped their confined spirits inside the human brain to permanently possess the minds of the Girgashite people. Once they were inside the limited confines of the human body they were forced to abide by physical laws. As time progressed, they forgot from whence they came and succumbed to the very instincts they had conditioned the Girgashite people to live under.

Before long, male Levites began to engage in sexual intercourse with captured female slaves. They engaged in orgies with female Levites and had multiple sex partners. As time progressed, the male

Levites continued to repeat their genetically inherited behavior and to conquer and divide and began to assimilate themselves within the indigenous races in the Mediterranean, and by AD 500, the Caucasians emerged. Following in the same footsteps, the male Caucasians continued to conquer and divide and soon spread throughout Europe. Soon, they too assimilated themselves within the Indigenous population and by AD 1300 brought forth the Anglo-Saxons of medieval Europe.

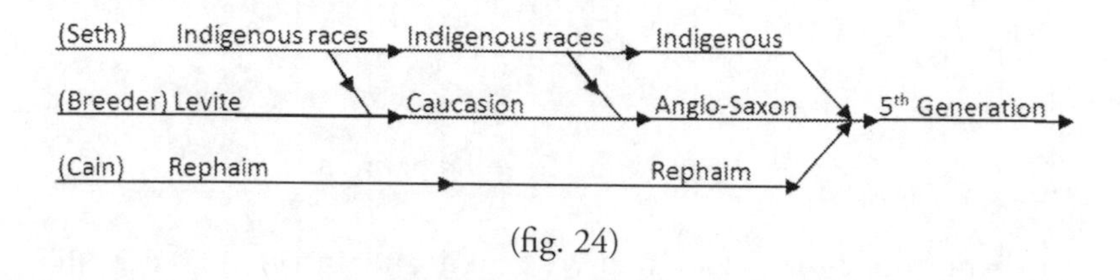

(fig. 24)

A Caucasian is a true descendant of a Levite. There is no mistake about this! Although the name Anglo-Saxon stands synonymous with the name Caucasian, this isn't true. The first Caucasian was never a European because he originated from the Caucas region as a Girgashite before he was conditioned to acquire a conscious mind. Later, he emerged in the Mediterrenean as a Levite with a human conscious. There exists no living person of Caucasian descent since the past 600 years because they assimilated into the Anglo-Saxon races. A Caucasian held the first genetic link to the Levite people but made no such claim. Historically, the ancient Greeks were the first Caucasians to establish a great empire.

An Anglo-Saxon is a European who shares a genetic link to a Caucasian. The modern Jewish race belongs to a small group of Anglo-Saxons who uphold a Jewish faith and who claim to be the descendants of the Hebrew people. A Hebrew was never a member of the human race! Although a male Hebrew shares a genetic link to the Amorite, he never mixed with the line of Seth or Cain; instead, he belongs to a line that derived from the Nation of Israel, and they originated from the fallen Sons of God and Isis.

The meaning for the name Anglo-Saxon does clarify one matter. In Latin, the word Anglo [angelo] implies an angel and, Saxon refers to the descendants of the sons of Isaac, and Isaac is the chosen progenitor to the human conscious; therefore, the name Anglo-Saxon derives from the angelic son of Isaac who descended from a Caucasian that came from a male Levite who in turn is a fallen angel that has possessed the body of a male Girgashite, and the Girgashite people descended from the nation of Israel, and they were chosen for the creation of the conscious mind through the scientific manipulation of El's spirit and of Afro-Asiatic genes. Now we know! The Seven Headed Serpent confined man's Michael spirit to a 13th dimension when it freed the El and Isis Spirits from the 14th and 15th dimensions.

Therefore, 2,400 years ago the human conscious was created the moment a spirit from El or Isis entered the frontal lobe of the left hemisphere of a male Girgashite brain; similarly, since the Caucasian and Indigenous races blended together, the human conscious has manifested when the Michael spirit in the human baby exists the right hemisphere to become entrapped inside the brain stem -- a process that becomes automatic and characterizes itself when a baby consciously attempts to pronounce words or letters.

Thus, intelligence as we know it originates from man's entrapped Michael spirit. Thought, as a process, becomes an electrical response from the human conscious to a stimulus that is received from one of the five senses. Memory – collective intelligence – originates from the conscious mind and becomes the storehouse for all experiences mental and physical that is recorded in the frontal lobe in the left hemisphere of the human brain. Man's entrapped Michael spirit understands the physical stimuli it receives through the brain stem when it uses the storehouse of conscious memory in the frontal lobe in the left hemisphere to sort out and make sense of the information.

In addition, human emotion also originates from the human conscious. Positive feelings of benevolence originate from man's Michael spirit; negative feelings of malevolence originate from man's El or Isis spirit located in the storehouse of conscious memory. The male Girgashite that was possessed by an El spirit was genetically programmed to have male offspring, and a male Girgashite that was possessed by an Isis spirit was genetically programmed to have female offspring. As a result, after conception, a male offspring possessed an El spirit, and a female, possessed an Isis spirit; however, this is not entirely 100% true, for the condition that is being referred to as homosexuality results when an El spirit resides within the female body or when an Isis spirit resides within the body of a male. It will be wise if we understand that homosexuality has been in existence since the human conscious was born, and that a person's choice of gender has nothing to do with his or her infinite Michael spirit but has everything to do with his or her finite El or Isis spirit on earth.

Furthermore, the human conscious became dependent upon a reflex action – an automatic and physical response from the human body that results before man's Michael spirit reacts to a physical stimulus. Man's entrapped Michael spirit responds either positive or negative to a reflex action. When it responds positive, man's Michael spirit becomes filled with a feeling of benevolence. When it responds negative, man's Michael spirit becomes filled with a feeling of malevolence.

Thus, the opposing forces of good and evil originate from the mind of man, but they were separated and delegated to belong to God and Satan respectively. Successfully and deceitfully, an Agenda has removed their presence from man's mind and separated them into two opposing entities. There is a reason, a purpose, for this diversion. By diverting responsibility away from the human conscious and projecting it toward God and Satan, an Agenda kept man clueless as to the origins of good and evil which is rooted within man himself as a by product of El and Isis.

For a change to follow, man is better served to handle his inner feelings. Once he realizes that good and evil exists within the framework of his own mind, he will be able to control his instinctive emotions, but since he continues to perceive evil as a source that originates from outside of his mind, his human psyche will continue to create the external forces called evil without eradicating the pervasive forces from his mind.

Spirit and consciousness, infinite consciousness and Michael spirit -- those are but a few of the terms we will use to define the human psyche. Spirit is the force of life energy that reverberates around two oxygen atoms to become the bond that holds them together to create the O2 molecule. When spirit becomes transferred, energy is released leaving only two oxygen atoms in its place. Consciousness is a state of responsiveness, a receptive state that allows the body of an animal to receive information then to react. If we remember our little baby from a previous discussion, before he uttered any words, he was in a state of consciousness. He experienced his world through his senses, so he saw, he heard, he felt, and tasted an object but couldn't understand what it was. Spirit brought forth the baby's consciousness as it brought life in the oxygen to his little body. Spirit represents a state the plants, the animals, and the human race are presently in.

Let's imagine a car (which we will compare to the human body); the car is turned on. While the car motor idles in park, it is alive and vibrant. We call this a state of consciousness. Now, while the car is in consciousness, it remains in a dormant and receptive state until a human conscious (a driver) sits behind the wheel to animate the car and drive it away. Spirit becomes the ignition that turns on consciousness. Although it ignites the body with life, spirit can't create intelligent thought, so man's Michael spirit, his intelligence, became the driver to change the gears of the human brain to allow for conscious thought to manifest.

In the case for the human race, when man's Michael spirit became entrapped in the brain stem, it was disconnected from the infinite consciousness and man's true identity, his subconscious, was lost. This disconnected the subconscious from man's Michael spirit. Infinite consciousness should never be confused with consciousness, for it stands as the minds void, the mental abyss that was created when man's Michael spirit severed itself from the original source of his identity. Infinite consciousness represents the large severed part of man's Michael spirit which connects to the Progenitor of the Universe; the subconscious becomes the other severed half of man's Michael spirit,

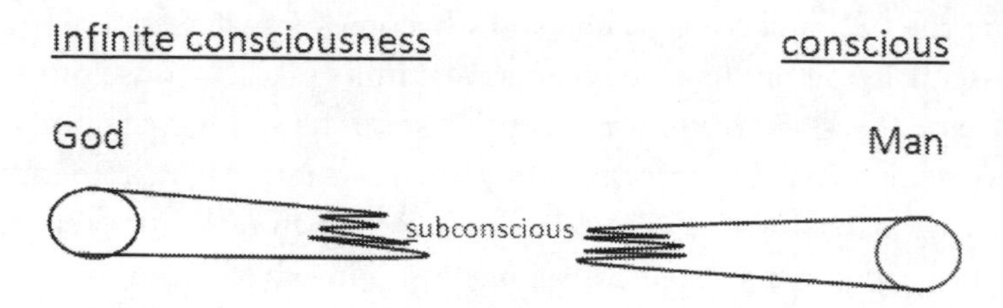

(fig. 25) Representation of man's severed Michael spirit.

and it stands responsible for the intricate and automatic functions of the human body, becoming man's hidden and inner-self. Because man knows virtually nothing about the subconscious and nothing about the infinite consciousness, he purposely and foolishly dubbed it "the subconscious mind."

Nothing comes closer to a lie! The subconscious stays above the level of the human conscious. Since it doesn't ever sleep, since it doesn't ever lie, since it runs and operates the human body with an immaculate precision and a pinpoint accuracy – the subconscious has to be a higher intelligence than the human conscious. If it daily partakes in rest (when man sleeps), if it lives an Agenda's lie, if it can't perform the intricate and complex functions of the human body which the subconscious continuously performs – the human conscious is at a level below the subconscious. Well, are the names reversed? Are we to continue living an Agenda's lie? Isn't the human conscious man's true subconscious, and isn't the subconscious man's true mind? Regardless of how we choose to surmise the matter, one fact becomes increasingly clear. The subconscious remains a baffling mystery which shows it to be an intelligence of unlimited potential. Virtually composed of super human power, it remains awake eternally, forever performing the intricate functions of the human body while providing subliminal messages to the human conscious. Another fact that distinguishes the subconscious from the conscious is truth. According to accepted guideline, the subconscious virtually never lies. Only when a person is a compulsive liar can the information from the subconscious be incorrect. For us, this comes as no surprise, for if the subconscious truly originates from the infinite consciousness, it is logical to presume that it is eternal and benevolent.

Meanwhile! The human conscious appears to be heading through a path to total annihilation thriving on sex and living for the grandeur of wealth and money. At the tender age of thirteen (puberty), the human conscious establishes a firm hold on man's Michael spirit loosening its grip by his mid-fifties (menopause); thus, the human conscious maintains a tight grip on the younger population group and through the use of the electronic media focuses on perverting through overemphasizing the material values of sex and money.

Isn't it to man's best interest to communicate with his subconscious, so he can understand his inner-self, his inner-most struggles, his inhibitions, his deepest fear. Man's subconscious belongs to his Michael spirit, and it originally formed his intelligence, and it was located within the frontal lobe of the right hemisphere. After El and Isis possessed the male Girgashite bodies, the brain stem became bombarded with sexual stimuli. To handle the bombardment, man's Michael spirit relocated in the brain stem. Because of the frequency and the magnitude of the incoming stimuli, man's Michael spirit became entrapped within the brain stem as it received and understood the information, and the spirit of El and Isis stood residing within the frontal lobe of the left hemisphere.

So the human conscience emerged to reciprocate between the spiritual forces of El or Isis in the frontal lobe in the left hemisphere and the Michael spirit in the brain stem. The human conscience originates from the subconscious and represents the only time the Progenitor of the Universe communicates to the conscious mind. Appearing in man's mind as a conscious thought, the conscience influences his ethical and moral behavior by instilling suggestions. People who commit heinous or extremely unethical or immoral acts of crime do so with no conscience (better known as remorse) because they willingly yet unknowingly disconnect their conscious mind from the conscience. Although the conscience communicates with man's conscious mind, the human conscious is prevented by the conscious mind from communicating with the conscience. In fact, it is through the conscience that the subconscious communicates with the conscious mind, so it stands to reason that it is through the conscience that man's entrapped Michael spirit communicates with the subconscious.

For this purpose, the conscience emerged to balance out the positive and negative forces in the human brain and to create what we will refer to as an average human mind. Because of the will and the benevolence from the Progenitor of the Universe, man has a rope to cling to prevent him from slipping further into the abyss we call the human conscious. The normal human being lies midway between the magnitudes of man's Michael spirit and his consciousness. If man's Michael spirit deviates toward consciousness, he inherits the sexual and instinctual impulses from the physical world. If man's Michael spirit deviates toward his subconscious, he inherits the spiritual forces from the subconscious

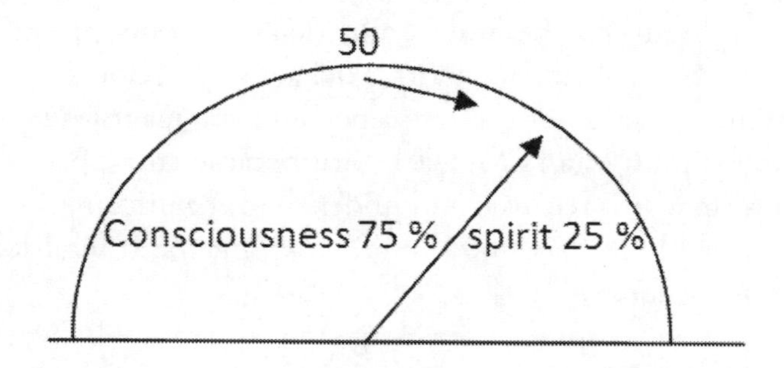

(fig. 26) 20th century man = 25 spirit\75 consciousness ratio.

Finally, and most importantly, there remains the subject of the Progenitor of the Universe – the impetus that started the universe in motion, the force from which the four physical forces originate, the intelligent order that permeates throughout the universe. As man attempted to comprehend a reality to the Progenitor of the Universe, it became impossible. By attempting to worship, to idolize, to explain the all-pervasive un-seen Force, man began to push himself away. Through his religions and his sciences, he fails to acknowledge an existence. As man innocently refers to the Progenitor of the Universe in a male gender, he has tragically and unknowingly pushed himself further away from the unseen, unknown, ever present and benevolent force. The Progenitor of the Universe is not a God. Nor, is the Progenitor of the Universe the Most High; not the Father nor his Son; not a He nor a She, if that matters. To inform the reader, those are the labels that man has attached to the fallen Nephilim and the fallen Huzin angels. The Progenitor of the Universe requests no thank-you or praise, no adoration or money. There remains by necessity one request, one simple act. Man is obliged to consciously make contact with his subconscious. By doing so, he will open a channel between the conscious (his entrapped Michael spirit) and the subconscious (his disconnected identity).

If man stops embracing the misconstrued labels that he has placed against the true God of the Universe, he will bring himself to accept the truth about his creator and the true God. He will understand that his sacred books have idolized false gods after all. Man will recognize the Progenitor of the Universe sent emissaries to earth to assist him through his current plight. The Bible calls them angels. Man calls them extraterrestrial. Regardless of what he chooses to label them, they are here ready to usher man into the new age. As meaningless and plight-less as life appears in this tumultuous 21st century, man can take comfort to know he is not alone, and as he is about to discover in the next chapter, the angels have created their own agenda to counteract an Agenda of a Snake.

CHAPTER SIX

The Ra Agenda

Time! What is it? Who created it? Since the moment man started to count time, he longed to find the answer, the truthful explanation to this age-old mystery. Man did not create the concept he calls time, nor did he create the calendar. Those two ideas were bequeathed to him by an Agenda of a Snake. Since the moment the calendar was introduced into human society, it became responsible for the spiritual degeneration of the human race.

Time! Who determined it? Is it a reality or is it an illusion? Earthly time was determined by the Sumerian people (4000B.C.) when they observed the motions and the phases from the moon as it orbits around the earth and then by the Egyptian people (3600 B.C.) who observed and measured the reciprocal movements from the sun as the earth rotates on its axis and revolves around it.

In respect to the changing positions from the sun, the rotation and the orbit from the earth creates an illusion to the observer who sees the sun move across the sky from east to west for a day then to see it disappear in the western horizon for a night only to watch it reappear in the eastern horizon on the next morning. In addition, the same observer sees the sun migrate from north to south during the fall and then from south to north during the spring.

To the observer on the earth, the sun's movements are caused by the reflection of the earth's movements. To the observer in outer space, when the North Star is used to fix the relative position of the earth to it, the earth rotates on its axis from west to east and revolves around the sun from south to north. Not only does the sun's movement become the opposite reflection of the movement from the earth, but any movement that comes from the sun constitutes total chaos in the solar system; thus, time as man perceives, is truly based on an illusion.

But why did man embrace time if it is an illusion? As an Agenda introduced the second family to the mating ritual, it used the calendar to deceive them into living within a finite reality. Preoccupied in his mundane affairs, man has little time to contemplate his true destiny, so he fell prey into the deliberate trap and latched on to the idea he calls time and used it to dictate his finite reality.

Beginning with the line of Cain and continuing to the fourth generation, man lives his life according to the laws that derive from a finite illusion. In today's time-ravaged world, there are three eight-hour groups that form an average person's 24 hours -- to sleep, to work, to relax. Those three groups form the conditioning factors that lead to the decline of spirituality in the human race. What appears as a weekend of relaxation will soon dissipate once man takes the time, to prepare his food, to bond with the family, to take care of the daily chores, to go to the temple; thus, man became conditioned to learn the truth behind his destiny he must visit the temple to praise and to worship alien gods.

The oldest calendar originated in 3760 B.C, in Nippur, in the land of ancient Sumer. There the Seven Headed Serpent introduced the lunar calendar (12x29.5= 354 days) To the Kenizzite (Sumerian) people. The Sumerian civilization remains the oldest on earth pre-dating Egypt by some 621 years. The Sumerians created the 12th signs in the zodiac. They understood the meaning of the new age which is 2,160 years long, and they applied the formula from the precession of the equinoxes to create the zodiac ages.

A complex mathematical formula was uncovered within the thousands of Mesopotamian tablets found among the ruins of King Ashurbanipal's great library at Nineveh excavated between the years 1848 and 1876. Known as the twelve signs in the zodiac, the formula measures the cyclical age of the precession through the shifts that occur in each of the 12 constellations. The formula for the Precession of the Equinoxes determines the cyclical wobble of the earth. Simply stated the earth's wobble begins at approximate zero degrees; it increases every 72 years by one degree. When the earth reaches the maximum wobble at approximate 30 degrees, the cyclical age (30x72=2,160 years) is complete. Precession,

Precession of the Equinoxes: Pisces

Degree	Long Count	Degree	Long Count
1	B.C. 49 + 72 =	17	1103 + 72 =
2	C.E. 23 + 72 =	18	1175 + 72 =
3	95 + 72 =	19	1247 + 72 =
4	167 + 72 =	20	1319 + 72 =
5	239 + 72 =	21	1391 + 72 =
6	311 + 72 =	22	1463 + 72 =
7	383 + 72 =	23	1535 + 72 =
8	455 + 72 =	24	1607 + 72 =
9	527 + 72 =	25	1679 + 72 =
10	599 + 72 =	26	1751 + 72 =
11	671 + 72 =	27	1823 + 72 =
12	743 + 72 =	28	1895 + 72 =
13	815 + 72 =	29	1967 + 54 =
14	887 + 72 =	31.5	2021 + 18 =
15	959 + 72 =	1	2039 = End Pisces
16	1031 + 72 =		

(fig 27)

the retardation of the earth's orbit around the sun, is caused by the earth's wobble which is increasing by one degree every 72 years. When the wobble reaches the 29th degree, it will reach the point of maximum intensity (called the degree of incident) which produces a slowing (precession) in the speed of the earth's orbit around the sun. The next shift in the wobble will cause the speed of the earth's orbit to decrease abruptly. This sudden change in the speed of the earth's orbit around the sun will allow the next observable shift in the sign in the zodiac to occur. The shift is witnessed precisely on the two longest days in the year -- the vernal and the autumnal equinoxes.

The Sumerians were aware of this phenomenon.

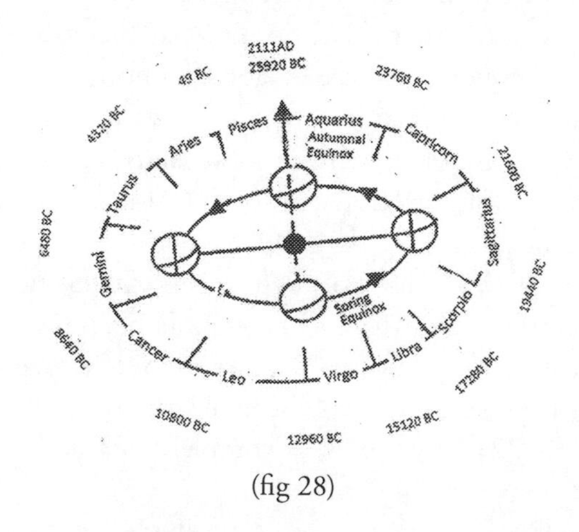

(fig 28)

They divided the circumference of the sky by the 12 constellations (the 12 houses in the zodiac) and allotted the 30 degrees in the wobble to each division, so the retardation (precession) to each house amounted to (12 x 30 =) 360 years.

Sacharia Sitchin "*When Time Began*" explains the mechanism behind this seemingly observable phenomenon, "because of the earth's tilt, it is just on these two days that the sun rises at the points where the celestial equator and the ecliptic circle intersect. Because of precession ... the zodiacal house in which this intersection occurs keeps shifting back appearing in a preceding one degree in the zodiacal band every seventy-two years. Although this point is still being referred to as the First Point in Aires, in fact we have been in the "Age" (or zodiac) of Pisces since about 60 B.C., and slowly but surely we will soon enter the Age of Aquarius. It is such a shift – the change from a fading zodiacal age to the start of another zodiacal age – that is the coming of a New Age."

To illustrate the effect precession will have on the observer, we compare the stillness in the background sky to the stillness on a stationary road; then, we compare twelve differently shaped and distantly spaced lines on the road to the twelve differently shaped and distantly spaced constellations in the sky. If a vehicle (we will call earth) moves forward at the right speed, the motion creates an optical illusion that makes the lines on the road (we will call constellations) appear to move backward. If the vehicle (earth) travels in a circular path (we will call orbit) while it maintains a semi-constant speed, the same twelve lines (constellations) will continue to appear at the precise intervals in time over and over again.

Now, if someone gazes up at the heaven on the designated day of the vernal or autumnal equinoxes – the longest days in the year – that person will observe a shift in the sign in the zodiac. Two thousand and eighty-eight years later a shift will occur that pushes the observable constellation backward away from sight (called the degree of incident) preparing for the next observable shift to occur within 72 years (the degree of maximum wobble). By 25,920 years (12 x 2,160), a complete cycle (known as the great year) occurs, and the phenomenon that man calls the zodiac will repeat itself over again.

By 3139 B.C., the Egyptians adapted the solar calendar (12x30=360 days) and dedicated it to their god Ra, and the editors of the book of Genesis marked that moment in time when the line of Seth and the line of Cain begin the process of spiritual digression through the union and then the implementation of the solar-lunar calendar.

Our conclusion for the age of the Egyptian Calendar is derived at by adding the ages of the first six patriarchs from Adam to derive at the total of 5,514 years.

Patriarch	Age
Adam	930
Seth	912
Enos	905
Cainan	910
Mahalaleel	895
Jared	962
Total	5514

(fig. 29)

Enoch's age of 365 (a solar year) is subtracted from the 5,514 to be left with 5,149 years ago which marks the year the Seven Headed Serpent introduced the Egyptian people to the solar calendar in 3138 B.C.

Lastly, around 2200 B.C. , at the start to the Age of Aires, the Kenite people adapted the system of calendars which history now chronicles as the Mayan Calendar Round. Known to man as the Tzolkin and the Haab, The oldest estimates places the Tzolkin in the sixth century B.C., and the Haab, it is speculated, appeared shortly afterwards. We will show that the Calendar Round began to count time from the beginning of the Age of Aires in 2111B.C. But first, there emerged another calendar that is attributed to the Maya culture that follows the Calendar Round and that leads mankind into the realm of apocalyptic revelation.

The Long Count Calendar begins counting time from the basic unit of measurement known as the kin. Current research determines the kin to reflect the period of one day. The kin is factored by the number 20 to produce 20 days; then, 20 days are factored by 18 to produce one winal (20x18 = 360 days). According to the current research, the number 360 is then factored by 20 to produce 7,200 days, and 7,200 is factored by 20 to produce 144,000 days and so on to produce the Long Count.

Date	Long Count	Days
0.0.0.0.1	1kin	1
0.0.0.1.0	1winal (20 kin)	20
0.0.1.0.0	1tun (18 winal)	360
0.1.0.0.0	1k'atun (20 tun)	7,200
1.0.0.0.0	1b'ak'tun (20 k'atun)	144,000

(fig. 30) Current research assumes the Long Count is a tally of days not years.

However, we contend that one kin reflects the period of 18 years. The kin or 18 years is factored not by the number 20 as the research presupposes, but by the double product (2) to produce (2x18 = 36 years) one winal. From this point forward, the Long Count takes a vital and crucial step in measuring the fate of humanity as it multiplies one winal by the celestial-product (10) to derive at one tun (10x36=360 years)

True Long Count	Years
1 kin	18
1winal (2 x 18)	36
1 tun (10 x 36)	360

(fig. 31) True Long Count consists of a tally of years not days.

Though it is the consensus and the opinion of the experts that the circumferential number of 360 reflects the days in the Long Count solar year -- it does not. The number 360 mathematically stands for the circumference of the earth. The number 36 which is one-half of the 72 years in the precession reflects the period in earthly time of 36 years, but the celestial-product (10 x 36) produces a period in celestial time of 360 years; therefore, we contend the Long Count Calendar and the phenomenon of the Precession of the Equinoxes are intricately interconnected one to the other.

Because the long Count and the precession are interconnected, it serves us no true purpose to interpret the Long Count through the information that has been gathered through the conventional research. Our sole objective is to highlight the significance the Long Count brings to the formula for the precession. Unbeknown to man is the fact, the long Count derived from the same formula that determines the precession.

The Ra Agenda understood this fact, and through the formula for the precession, they calculated the earth's wobble and demonstrated, mathematically, that over the period of many years it increases from approximate zero to approximately 30 degrees and that it increases by one degree for every 72 years; therefore, the cyclical age, according to the formula for the precession, is precisely 2,160 years long.

When the formula for the Precession of the Equinoxes is divided by the number four and compared side by side to the conventional formula for the long Count, there is an identical pattern that is present in their numbers.

Precession	**Years**	**True Long Count**	**Years - Epoch**
.25 degree =	18 =	1 kin =18 x10 =	180 1/12 age
.5 degree =	36 =	1 winal = 36 1tun = 36 x 10 =	360 1/6 age
1 degree =	72 =	1 k'atun = 72 x10 =	720 1/3 age
2 degree =	144 =	1b'ak'tun = 144 x10 =	1,440 2/3 age
3 degree =	216 =	cyclical age = 216 x10	2,160 3/3 age

(fig. 32) Mathematical correlations that exist between the Precession and the Long Count can be best appreciated when both are divided by four..

The pattern differs only in the position of the factors 2 x 18 years for the precession and in 20 days x 18 days for the Long Count. Researchers not only mistake the number of years in the precession to represent the number of days in the Long Count, but also, the research misplaces the values. Current research mistakes the double factor for the number of years and the number of years it mistakes for the double factor. In addition, current research multiplies the celestial factor 10 to the double factor (2) to produce 20 days which is factored by eighteen. This error hidden deep within the Long Count differs only by the number of zeros between the decimal places. To the Long count, the numbers represent earthly time; to the precession, they represent celestial. But in order to correlate the two, the kin must be divided by the number four to reduce it to 0.25 kin; the one degree in the Precession must be divided by four to convert it to a decimal of 0.25, and the 72 years must be reduced into the factor eighteen.

As both sides are compared to the equation,

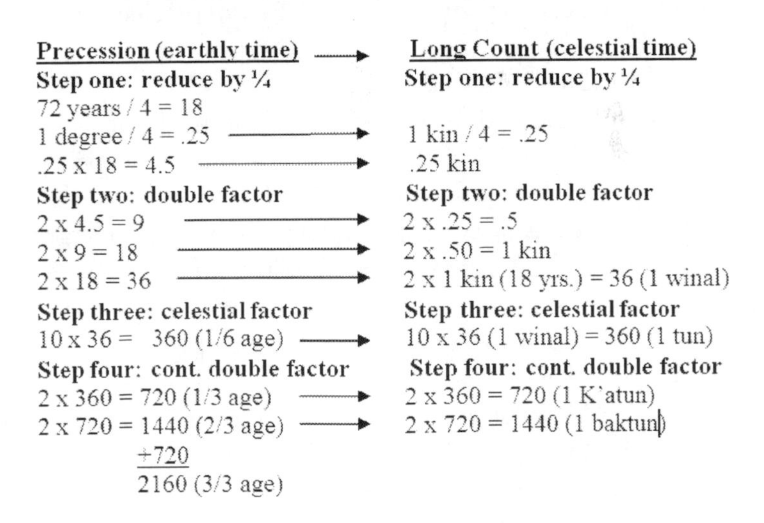

(fig. 33) The conversion formula converts Precession (earthly) to celestial (Mayan) time.

we discover that the multiple of 4.5 years in the Precession conforms to 0.25 kin in the Long Count. When the double product is introduced, we learn that 18 years in the Precession conforms to one kin. We can also conclude, through the use of the double product, that 36 years is equal to one winal, and when the celestial product is introduced, 360 years becomes equal to one tun. When both sides to the equation become factored by the number ten, we derive at the celestial product of 360 and at the equation which converts celestial into earthly time.

Once the double product is factored to the celestial product (2x360 =720) to both sides of the equation, we arrive at the time that is designated by the precession to represent the first-third of the Age of Pisces, and when the double product is factored to the celestial co-product (2x720 = 1,440), we arrive at the time designated by the precession to represent two-thirds of the Age of Pisces. To finalize this inquiry, we subtracted 1,440 from the cyclical age 2160 to derive at 720 years which represent the last third of the Age of Pisces; thus, the factor (3x720) is equal to the cyclical age divided by three. The Long Count enables man to measure the enormous length of time within the Age of Pisces dividing it threefold into the cyclical age.

Earlier, we introduced the zodiac ages. We learned that the cyclical age coincides with a visible shift in the sign in the zodiac. In chapter four, we compared the first four ages in the Mayan Calendar to the four generations in the book of Genesis, and we observed the emergence of the human race coincides chronologically with the first Age of Gemini, so it reasons the Mayan Calendar Round and the Long Count play a crucial and vital role to determine the fate of humanity.

Much attention has been focused on the Long Count since it is causing quite a stir among the public consensus about the end times. For the moment it becomes sufficient to say, the Long Count highlights the four previous cyclical ages through the signs in the zodiac and delineates the fifth age to the coming Age of Aquarius.

Man in the 21st century determines time through the illusory movements from the sun and the moon. But the Mayans didn't! They incorporated the system of calendars that measures earthly time by determining the physical wobble in the earth. As we can ascertain, any attempt that someone undertakes to interpret the Long Count through the use of earthly time shall be futile, for the Long Count determines time on earth by dividing the zodiacal Age of Pisces by the phenomenon which is handed down to man and is known as the Precession of the Equinoxes.

Precession is the mechanism by which author Zecharia Sitchin "*The Earth chronicles*" determines as celestial time. Spirits use the cyclical ages through precession to track earthly time. Although they come from another dimension, so time is inconsequential to them, they use the precession to relate to the events on earth. The period in the Long Count, as we discovered in chapter four, is equal to an astounding 10,000 years; thus, the 20 periods in the Long Count Calendar represent 20 days in celestial time or 200,000 years, and the five ages that are highlighted in the Long Count comprise the 21st period -- the last celestial day (10,000 years) In which the creation of the human race occurs.

After the flood, as the second generation multiplied and proliferated on the earth, the Kenite people (descendants of Japheth) used the Calendar Round to convert the precession into earthly time for the Age of Aires. They began by counting forward in time going backward through the cyclical Age of Aires. The end of the 21st century for Aires becomes the beginning of the 1st century for Pisces.

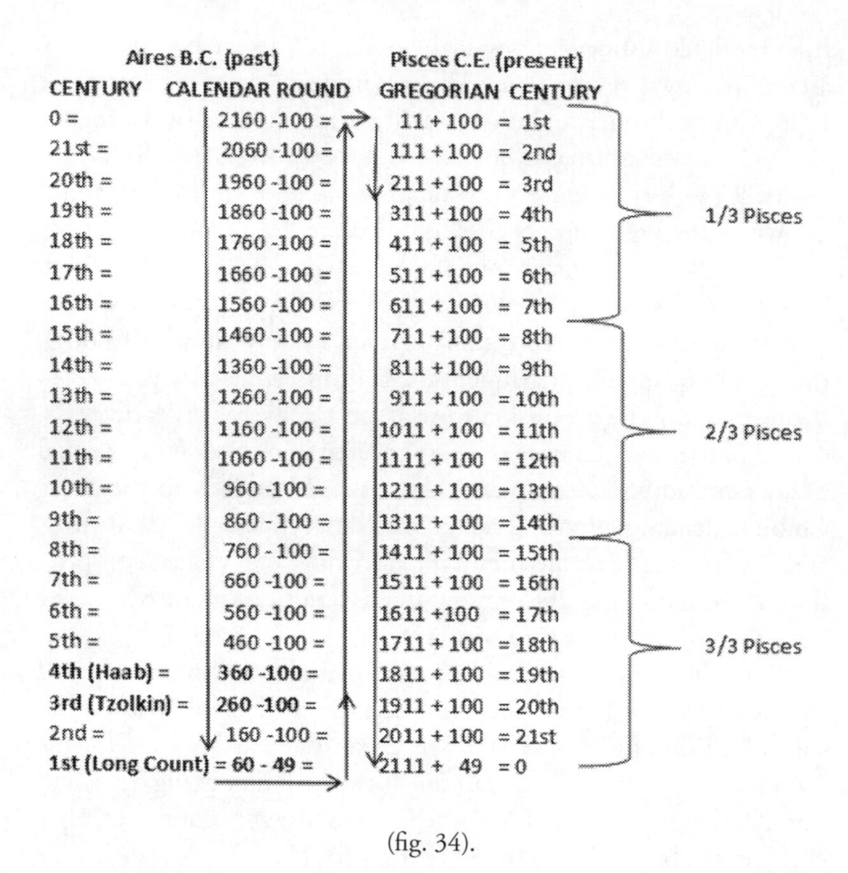

Aires B.C. (past)		Pisces C.E. (present)	
CENTURY	CALENDAR ROUND	GREGORIAN CENTURY	
0 =	2160 -100 =	11 + 100 = 1st	
21st =	2060 -100 =	111 + 100 = 2nd	
20th =	1960 -100 =	211 + 100 = 3rd	
19th =	1860 -100 =	311 + 100 = 4th	1/3 Pisces
18th =	1760 -100 =	411 + 100 = 5th	
17th =	1660 -100 =	511 + 100 = 6th	
16th =	1560 -100 =	611 + 100 = 7th	
15th =	1460 -100 =	711 + 100 = 8th	
14th =	1360 -100 =	811 + 100 = 9th	
13th =	1260 -100 =	911 + 100 = 10th	
12th =	1160 -100 =	1011 + 100 = 11th	2/3 Pisces
11th =	1060 -100 =	1111 + 100 = 12th	
10th =	960 -100 =	1211 + 100 = 13th	
9th =	860 - 100 =	1311 + 100 = 14th	
8th =	760 - 100 =	1411 + 100 = 15th	
7th =	660 -100 =	1511 + 100 = 16th	
6th =	560 -100 =	1611 +100 = 17th	
5th =	460 -100 =	1711 + 100 = 18th	3/3 Pisces
4th (Haab) =	**360 -100 =**	1811 + 100 = 19th	
3rd (Tzolkin) =	**260 -100 =**	1911 + 100 = 20th	
2nd =	160 -100 =	2011 + 100 = 21st	
1st (Long Count) =	**60 - 49 =**	2111 + 49 = 0	

(fig. 34).

The calendar continues to descend by century until it reaches the end of the 4th (360) and the end of the 3rd (260). There it reveals the fact of a mistaken identity: the Haab (360) and the Tzolkin (260) are not calendars at all; they are the 4th and 3rd centuries from the Age of Aires.

The formula [20 (x+5)] was used by the Mayans to count forward in time through the centuries while traveling backward in time through Aires. Thus, the second century computes to 20 x (3+5) = 160, and the first century becomes 20 x 3 = 60. The Tzolk'in (20 x 13) which is 20 x (8+5) and the Haab (20 x 18) which is 20 x (13+5) are multiples that derive from the formula [20 (x + 5)]. Once the calendar reaches the last 60 years of the 1st century, 49 years are subtracted from the last 60 years to compensate for the birth of Jesus which occurred 49 years before the Age of Pisces began. Thus, the Age of Pisces begins in 49 B.C.

Total years in Age of Pisces	2160
Mayan 21st century (2011)	-2111
Birth of Jesus	49 B.C.

(fig. 35).

If the total number of years from the Haab is subtracted from the cyclical age (2,160-360), the 19th century, which marks the beginning of the 1800s, will emerge. This period indicates the time when the degree of incident in the earth's wobble is reached. If the total number of years from the Tzolkin is subtracted from the cyclical age (2,160-260), the 20th century, which marks the beginning of the 1900s, will emerge. This period indicates the time when the slowing in the earth's orbit takes place. If the 160 years that belong to the following century in the Calendar Round is subtracted from the cyclical age (2,160-160), the 21st century, which marks the beginning of the year 2000, will emerge. This period marks the end for the 2nd century of Aires and the start for the 21st century of Pisces.

CENTURY	CALENDAR ROUND	GREGORIAN CENTURY		
5th =	460 -100 =	1711 + 100	= 18th	
4th (Haab) =	**360 -100 =**	1811 + 100	**= 19th**	**degree of incident**
3rd (Tzolkin) =	**260 -100 =**	1911 + 100	**= 20th**	**1st precession**
2nd =	**160 -100 =**	2011 + 100	**= 21st**	**begin 21st century**
1st (Long Count) =	**60 - 49 =**	2111 + 49	**= 0**	**degree of maximum wobble**

(fig. 36).

Now, if the 2011 years that have elapsed from this Common Era are subtracted from the 2160 years in the Age of Pisces, there will be exactly 149 years remaining. But this deduction is far from being correct. The 149 years that remain come as the result from the discrepancy that occurred when the Calendar Round and the Long Count were formulated to coincide with the Gregorian calendar. One hundred years must be deducted from the 149 years to compensate for the Calendar Round which began counting time 100 years after 11 B.C. This leaves 49 years that remain. But there are 18 years that are lost when the conversion formula (18 x 0.25 = 4.5; then, 4.5 x 2 = 9) is applied. This leaves the Long Count counting time in 2 B. C. – 9 years after the Age of Pisces begins. We subtract 9 years from 49 which leaves the count at 40 years. But the Age of Pisces began in 11 B.C., so we must subtract 11 years from 40 (40-11=29) to compensate for the 11 years in the Long Count which leaves the Age of Aquarius to start in the year 2040 (2011+29) of the Common Era.

Cyclical age - 21st century	2160 - 2011 = 149
Years remaining - discrepancy (C.R.)	149 - 100 = 49
Years remaining - discrepancy Long Count	49 - 9 = 40
Years remaining - discrepancy Gregorian	40 - 11 = 29
Years remaining in Pisces	29

(fig. 37).

To understand the reason for why natural catastrophes continue to rise in frequency and magnitude since the past nine years, man needs to examine, not the Mayan calendar, but the Precession of the Equinoxes, for as we have already mathematically demonstrated, they are intricately interconnected.

According to the formula for the long Count which converts earthly time to the Precession, if a shift of one degree occurs in the wobble of the earth, precession will measure 72 years, and the Long Count will measure 10 x 72 = 720 or one tun which measures 1/3 of the Age of Pisces; if a shift of 2 degrees occurs in 144 years in the precession, the Long Count will measure 10 x 144 = 1,440 years or one katun which measures 2/3 of Aires, and if a shift of 3 degrees occurs in 216 years in the precession, the Long Count will measure 10 x 216 = 2,160 years or 3/3 of the Age of Aires.

Precession	Years	True Long Count	Years
1 degree	72	10 x 72	720
2 degrees	144	10 x 144	1, 440
3 degrees	216	10 x 216	2, 160

(fig. 38).

This means that by the year 1967, the earth's wobble had already shifted to the all-significant 29 degrees,

	Precession of the Equinoxes: Pisces	
	Degree	**Long Count**
(Haab)	28	1895 + 72 = degree of incident
(Tzolkin)	29	1967 + 54 = 1st precession
End 21st cent.	31.5	2021 + 18 = maximum wobble
Long Count	1	2039 = End Pisces

(fig. 39)

Cyclical age - end Pisces	2160 – 2039 = 121
Remaining years / by double-factor	121 / 2 = 60.5
Remaining years - birth of Jesus	60.5 - 49 = 11.5
Remaining years - discrepancy L.C.	11.5 - 9 = 2.5 shift to occur in 2021
2.5 shift / by celestial-factor	2.5 / 10 = .25 degree

(fig. 40) Formula for the Precession and the Long Count reversed to indicate final 2.5 shift.

and the speed of the earth's orbit around the sun experienced its first decrease. Interestingly, in 1960 the strongest earthquake to date of a 9.5 magnitude occurred in southern Chile which also triggered a tsunami, and in 1964 the second strongest earthquake in history of a 9.2 magnitude occurred in Prince William Sound, Alaska. These two record-making earthquakes fall within seven years from the year 1967 when the wobble of the earth had reached the 29th degree of incident.

In order to determine the midway point between 72 years or one katun, the Mayans incorporated the tun or 36 years. If one tun is added to the year 1967, the result will be the year 1967+36= 2003. Mankind had reached the half-way point, the last 36 years that remain in the Age of Pisces. Curiously enough, the third biggest earthquake in history occurred on the very next year of 2004: a 9.0 magnitude earthquake occurred of the Indonesian island of Sumatra which triggered a deadly tsunami and killed 226,000 people.

To determine the halfway point between 36 years or one tun, the Mayans incorporated the kin or 18 years. If one kin is added to the year 2003, the resulting sum will be the year 2021. At first glance, this year appears to be insignificant, but when the numerals for the number 21 are interchanged, the result becomes the highly publicized year of 2012.

The calculation which determines the date December 21, 2012 which is theorized will represent the end of the world is derived at by using the Goodman/Martinez correlation of the Long Count which fixes the date August 11, 3114 B.C. as the chronological starting point for the Long Count calendar. But since the Long Count started counting time for the cyclical Age called Pisces in the year 11 B.C., the GMT correlation started counting time from 3114 B.C. to the present without compensating for the nine years that are lost when the conversion formula (18 x 0.25=4.5x2) is used. So nine years must be added to the highly awaited and highly publicized year of 2012 to derive at the unknown but no less spectacular year of 2021.

This interchangeability between the numbers 12 and 21 isn't a coincidence. The final shift in the wobble of the earth which is supposed to happen in 2039 will occur 18 years prematurely in the year 2021. This final wobble will shift not by one, but by two point five degrees. This abrupt shift is set to occur not in 2012 but in

2021 and it signifies not the end of the world, but the start to the final age for mankind the Age of Aquarius. The Mayans fore-told this celestial phenomenon not as an event that will mark the end of the world, but as an event that will culminate the end of the Age of Pisces and will introduce the final kin that remains before the new age begins.

The catastrophic but natural events that man continues to experience during the Age of Pisces will be absent from the 18 years that will remain after the final shift occurs. In the meantime, mankind will continue to experience a bombardment in the frequency and magnitude of these natural occurrences until they culminate into several mayor events in the year twenty-twenty one. At that point, the 2.5 degree shift will bring the earth's maximum wobble to 31.5 degrees and will cause the speed of the earth's orbit around the sun to decrease significantly. When the two phenomenon occur, the energy released from the friction caused from the movements of the tectonic plates will create a series of tsunamis triggered by the series of earthquakes. Within four and one-half years, mid-way into the year 2025, the speed of the earth's orbit around the sun will return to normal. By the year 2040, the wobble of the earth will become one degree and the cyclical Age called the zodiac of Aquarius will officially begin.

Does it become clear! Had we already known! No man could create the complex mathematical system he calls the signs in the zodiac if no human could continuously-observe the 72 year-long shift. Are we to believe ancient man created a complex and ingenious system that determines ages he could never see or measure periods in time he could never experience, and, "if that isn't hard enough to swallow" he left behind the Mayan system of calendars to affirm this knowledge to the future generations that will follow. This assertion, in itself, becomes preposterous!

There can be only one logical explanation, only one definite and clear-cut conclusion which man can draw upon. The monument, he calls the Long Count Calendar, is bestowed to him by intelligences that are capable of observing the shifts in the signs in the zodiac. Although ancient man divided the sky allotting to it the twelve signs in the zodiac in the attempt to measure the ages, it was the spirits who departed from earth some 4,000 years ago and who imparted to mankind the Mayan system of calendars to affirm that they -- the Ra Agenda – were here on planet earth.

Since time, as we perceive, occurs slowly for spirits but expeditiously for man, Spirits use the precession to track time on earth. As incredulous as this statement may appear, 10,000 years in human history becomes equivalent to a single celestial period in the Long Count Calendar. From pure curiosity we divided 2,160 years into 10,000 years to derive at the decimal of 4.6; hence, on earth, a spirit experiences four ages and three-fifths into the fifth age in the celestial period. Now, for the sake of clarity, we divided the number four representing the four preceding ages in the Long Count into the 24 hour period in a day to derive at the dividend of six celestial hours. Therefore, for every six hours that elapses in the celestial period, the spirit on earth observes the shift in the sign in the zodiac that becomes associated with the coming of the new age.

Since time runs expeditiously for man and slowly for the spirits, it leaves a gap in between. Because of this gap, this insurmountable difference between earthly and celestial time, the Ra Agenda could foretell the future for mankind, and through the Mayan Calendar Round and the Long Count coupled with the biblical book of Genesis, they foretold the arrival of the fourth generation which would come at the beginning of the Age of Pisces and of the arrival of the fifth generation which was to occur at the beginning of the Age of Aquarius; thus, the Calendar Round informed man about the degradation in the level of awareness in the spirit in human consciousness that was to come in the Age of Pisces coupled with the increase in material consciousness. The Long Count informed mankind about the increase in the level of awareness in the spirit of human consciousness that has become so evident in the year 2011 but will become complete by the year twenty-forty.

Of the five ages in the Long Count, four of them foretold the events that lead to the creation of the human race. Man stands poised ready to enter into the fifth and final age in the year twenty-forty. By the year 2012, man will begin to experience the rebirth to his subconscious awareness and will begin to demand social and political reform. No longer shall he choose to accept the dire consequences to his unfortunate fate simply because he is conditioned to do so. By the year 2040, for the first time in modern human history, man will begin to unite as a species and to shatter the bonds to the conditioning processes that have destabilized his human spirit since the past 2,100 years.

Fortuitously for man, the spirits of El and Isis perverted his mind by introducing him to the mating ritual and conditioned his human spirit to embrace the desire for the need of money. As a consequence to his misfortune, man became driven by the will of the sexual impulse and became dictated by the greed for money. Those two influences – lust for sex and lust for money – are rooted from the start with El and Isis and are the two forces that influence and bombard the human conscious of virtually every living human being.

In addition, man's disgrace comes through the untimely mishap which occurred when the Anglo-Saxon races, which are genetically descended from the Caucasian, inherited the power, the wealth, and the human conscious. But the Indigenous races, which are genetically descended from Malek, inherited the biblical curse of Canaan.

The Indigenous people lived all over the world and lived according to the will of the Michael spirit which require of them to live in balance with the natural environment and to live in tune with the internal and external forces of nature. But in the 15th Century, the Europeans invaded the New World and used the conscious mind to control and to oppress the Indigenous people. History has narrated for man the rest! The untold story of El and Isis has driven the human race into a downward spiral of spiritual digression!

Therefore, the fifth age foretold of a remote time in the Age of Aquarius when the Elohim will descend from the moon's first dimension accompanied by the 144, 000 un-fallen Sons of God. Together, they along with the princes of light (the Ra Agenda) will wage a defensive, an ongoing protection for the children of the light (the fifth generation) against the princes who fell into the darkness and who reign incarnate on planet earth as an Agenda of a Snake. There is hope!

Thus, the fourth age foretold of a time when the Levite, through his inherited traits from El and Isis, the Caucasian, and the Anglo-Saxon, through the natural course of time, mixed themselves through natural breeding with the African and the Indigenous races. If we take the ages (breeding times) of the first two patriarchs and add them together, we discover that it took approximately 1,800 years to breed the Sumerian and the Egyptian people before the second family emerged. Likewise, it took the fourth generation 1,800 years to breed and to reach fruition some 300 years ago, but the fifth generation, which has yet to bloom, has only begun to breed within the womb of the 21st century.

For the Ra Agenda, the fifth generation signifies a new era that will introduce the new age that will begin to slowly progress man's Michael spirit back to the position from where it originated. Yes – it is true! By a curious yet unknown set of circumstances, children who are born since the year 2000 have the Michael spirit to consciousness ratio set at 65 to 35 percent.

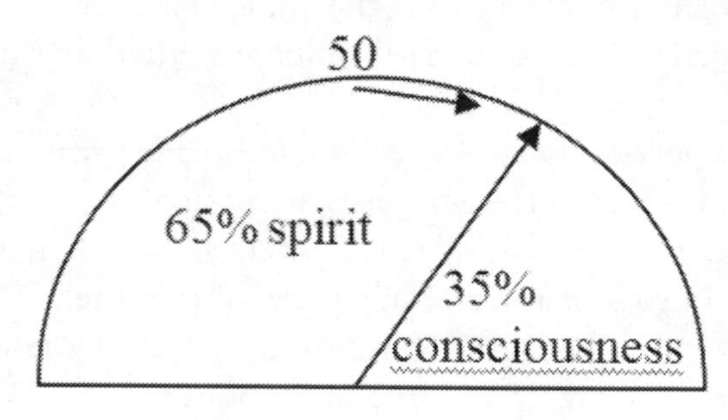

(fig. 41) Conscious awareness of the Fifth Generation.

This increase, in the spirit ratio, reflects the condition where man's entrapped human spirit has begun to slowly free itself from the brain stem to begin the journey to the frontal lobe of the right hemisphere. This condition has slowly begun to manifest in the human race since the year two thousand and eight.

The Long Count Calendar fore-tells a time when the Cherubim Michael, Ra, and Viracocha will consult with the Elohim to create a time-line from which to make contact with specific people from the human race. The time-line began in 1955 and will end in the year twenty thirty-nine. The cherubim from Pluto (Michael) and from Jupiter (Ra) and from Mars (Viracocha) are coming to earth to prepare the global human society for a beginning to the end from the clutches of an Agenda of a Snake.

Since the past 2,500 years, an Agenda of a Snake comprises itself from the group of families who genetically but historically remain connected. Since 2008, they have lost the control of the world governments and financial institutions. Through their inherent greed, corruption, and deceit, those families, who manipulated the world's economy through an Agenda, have lost their grip on the governments and financial institutions of the world.

Now, as man stands at the doorstep to the Age of Aquarius, the Cherubim Michael, Ra, and Viracocha intensified their visits to earth. They show the surmounting interest to examine the global human society but show no desire to establish contact with any of the officials from the world governments. Instead, the angels began to establish contact with a chosen group of people that is being selected from the unique and diverse societies on planet earth.

But if aliens and angels have established contact with the human species, wouldn't man know, at least from the subconscious level, how *E.T.* looks? Well, this logic isn't exactly correct. Man has yet to realize how arrogant, how self-centered, he has come to be to foolishly assume that *E.T.* possesses the material form simply because he possesses the physical body.

For the sake of clarity, we constructed a hypothetical analogy. We challenged the old but familiar notion the human being is the highest species of animal on earth, for we believe that he sits at the low end to the scale of life. Man belongs to the animal kingdom, and the animal exists by way of consciousness. However, while the animal obeys nature's laws and lives through the infinite consciousness, man doesn't, because he lives in the conscious; while the animal evolved into a biological life-form without the spirit, the human being evolved into a genetically manipulated life-form created through the spirit of the fallen angel, and while the animal reaches its destiny and lives in total harmony with the laws of nature, man is deprived of his spiritual destiny and is conditioned to defy the laws of nature; therefore, since the animal becomes Michael's creation, man becomes Satan's creation. Accordingly, the animal sits higher in the scale of life than the human. Indeed, we are saddened, sorry (since we include ourselves in this rather inclusive category) to learn the only life-forms that man is higher than in the scale of life are rodents, roaches, and flies. So the truth spilled out! And we uncovered there is nothing sacred about man! He is the entrapped embodiment of the Isis and Elite spirits that comprise the human body, and his Michael spirit resides inside the brain of an animal. He has become the most degenerated animal life on planet earth.

Since the word human originates from the name of the Huzinite, and since the Hu(zin)man comes from the womb of Isis, he became known as a wo(mb)man – a man that derived from the womb of the Huzinite. The word woman never did refer to the feminine gender, for in the Bible, the female derives from the rib of Adam, so Eve would be called a rib-man. Instead, we found the word female derives its roots from the feminine name of Malek. Through the natural course of time, the name Male(k) became shortened to male to refer to the masculine Malek and to female to refer to the fe(minine) Male(k). For what purpose did we play on the important meaning of these words, simply to inform the reader, aliens or angels couldn't possibly possess physical bodies because they are not animals! Aliens possess a semi-corporeal form that is partially visible to the naked eye. Angels possess an incorporeal form that is invisible to the naked eye. They are spirits who come to earth from the incorporeal to the corporeal realm.

Since they live in a dimension different than the animals, spirits live in a dimension different than man, for he resides in earth's 13th dimension, the dimension of consciousness which is better known to him as the three dimensional world. Aliens reside in the fifth dimension, the dimension of spirit which becomes known to man as the subconscious world.

The difference between the fifth and the thirteenth dimension became due to the higher rate of vibration. Matter that comes from the corporeal world vibrates at a rate much slower than matter that comes from the incorporeal world; as a result, the planets and the satellites contain a total of fifteen dimensions each, and matter that comes from the fifteenth dimension vibrates at a slower rate than matter that comes from the first. Since angels come from the first dimension and aliens come from the fifth (the fifth being a slower vibratory realm than the first but a higher vibratory realm than the three dimensional world), they cannot establish physical contact with the human being.

So the question still lingers. How does the alien look? If we stop to examine the bizarre array of alien characters that have been depicted on the screen, there will develop the traditional depiction of the so-called gray: a three and a half to four and a half feet humanoid being with an oversized head, large eyes that are deep set slightly slanted and far apart, no ear lobes, no formed nose (nares only), a slit for a mouth, thin arms and legs, hands that have four fingers (two double length from the other), and a tough gray skin.

The story that lies behind this traditional depiction

(Figure 42) Artificial life-form

emerges from the UFO abduction experience. The first record in the U.S. of an alien abduction occurred in 1961. Betty and Barney Hill, a married interracial couple, were driving on Route three south of Lancaster, New Hamsphire. They were keeping an eye on an object that was following them for some time from out in the near distance. The object was cigar shaped and appeared to have red, amber, green, and blue lights rotating around it. Betty and Barney Hill did not here a sound coming from the UFO. It was early in the morning, and they were tired, isolated within the lonely stretch of road. The object stopped almost directly ahead of them a few hundred feet high. The UFO was huge and had a double row of windows. Barney stopped the car in the middle of the road. He scrambled out of the car with the motor still running and Betty sitting in the passenger side. With binoculars in his hands, he was attempting to identify the strange object. By now, the object had moved closer to the car about a short city block away. Barney described it as pancake shaped. Through his binoculars he saw a double row of windows and six beings who were staring at him. Barney panicked. He jumped back in the car. Speeding off the road, Barney shouted to Betty, "we're going to be captured." They heard a strange electronic beeping coming from the trunk (beep, beep--beep,beep,beep). The car seemed to vibrate. They felt an odd-tingling sensation, and drowsiness came over them. Sometime later, the beeping sound returned. They were still in the moving car and Barney was at the wheel. They saw a sign-post Indian Head to Ashland. Their watches had stopped working at about five A.M. When they arrived home, the couple remained confused as to why it took them four hours to complete a trip that should have taken two. Soon Barney began to experience nightmares, and he developed a debilitating ulcer. Fearing that Barney's medical condition was associated with the UFO experience, the couple required the services of a psychologist named Benjamin Simon to help them explain why they could not account for the two hours in missing time. Betty and Barney Hill had lost the first two hours of their conscious memory since the moment they encountered the light. Months later, to their surprise, Dr Simon played for them the tape composite of their separate hypnotic regressions. Barney's ulcer disappeared, and Betty and Barney Hill came to accept the two hours of missing time and to realize the truth to the reality of their UFO experience.

The 70's and 80's would bring forth the bulk of the UFO abduction cases. By the 90's, UFO abductions would take a dramatic turn: the alien s appeared to be taking human samples of egg and sperm. Then, hypnotist/UFO researcher Bud Hopkins through his case studies wrote "*Abduction*" and "*Missing Time*" and introduced the composite drawings of *E.T.* as seen through the subconscious world of the UFO abduction experience literally bringing *E.T.* into the family living room. Before long other books on abductions followed, but the event that leads man to describe those strange small humanoids lies buttressing itself within the most unbelievable event in modern human history – the Roswell incident.

July 8, 1947, Roswell Army Base in Roswell, New Mexico, the public information officer at the base, Walter Haut, issued the following release to the press without obtaining authorization from the base commander Colonel William Blanchard, "Air Force recovers disc from rancher." He went on to say the rancher stored the disc, and the Army sent Jessie A. Marcel from the 509th Bomb Group Intelligence Office to recover the wreckage. Less than 24 hours later, the Army released a new story: the disc was nothing more than a crashed weather balloon. But the buzz within the Army base had immediately begun, and it told of some six creatures and a crashed disc that were recovered at another site. Many years passed and the Roswell event had all but been forgotten before the testimony from key eyewitnesses began to surface. These witnesses had confidential ties to the memorable experience, and they began to relate a different story.

In the book "*The Roswell Incident*" author s Conrad and Mo ore reveal, through the testimony from key eye-witnesses and the surviving data that is available, that not one but two separate incidents occurred that day. Key eyewitnesses, who were forever tied to the memorable event, confirmed the U.S. Army immediately implemented a code of top secret obliging them to remain silent. And they did. But in their advanced ages, the eyewitnesses (some near their deathbed) began to confess their experiences. What a story they told! Through the testimonies, the story of a government cover-up emerged. The witnesses told how the United States Government recovered dead aliens from the second wreckage to secretly escort the bodies away. There is no question that an event of such magnitude to attract the attention from the media worldwide occurred in New Mexico in July of nineteen forty-seven. *The Roswell Incident* provides the testimony that becomes necessary to take the cover-up at a face value, but we contend that it is theoretically impossible for a UFO to crash and to kill the aliens that are inside because aliens can't experience physical death.

But if aliens don't die and if the Roswell legacy is to remain the true and the historic event that is imprinted upon history – what happened at Roswell? Well, let's, for a moment, consider the circumstance. Let's suppose some highly important and distinguished visitor enters unannounced into your front yard. He walks straight up to the doorstep and rings the door bell. He has come to deliver a very important message that is graciously sent to you, granting you an exclusive offer. Due to circumstances beyond the messenger's control, he can only visit for a few seconds. However, because consciously you have a fear of him, you pay the messenger no mind. You ignore the ringing door-bell and you continue on as though he isn't there. Although the distinguished emissary knows that you are in denial and in fear of him, he rings the doorbell several times in the hope to establish contact with you. After several seconds tick by, he leaves a calling card at your door. The simplest message which can be conveyed by him that appears remotely complex to you: **I Was Here**!

Did the Roswell legacy become a calling card perpetrated by the Ra Agenda? Is the wreckage that is presumed to come from the crashed UFO an ejected capsule, and are the dead bodies that are presumed to be recovered by the U.S. military the spiritless bodies of the artificial life-form? Is history right but wrong at the same time? Yes! A supernatural outer-worldly experience did occur at Roswell. The testimonies that come from the group of eye-witnesses attest to this fact. But No! The officials from the United States Government didn't recover any dead aliens even though they believe they did.

The spirit inside the UFO is a non-corporeal life-form who uses the corporeal (artificial) life-form to establish physical contact with the human being. The artificial life-form is a biologically created android that is capable of performing intricate and delicate scientific procedures inside the UFO. In the decade of the 1980s, the image of the artificial life-form came to represent *E.T.* It appears as the alien that performs physical examinations on the helpless human subjects; it measures three and a half to four and a half feet tall and has large sensors (eyes) and a gray or green color. In one hundred percent of the UFO abduction s, the artificial life-form makes direct contact with the human subject. Whenever someone sees the depiction of a three-foot alien, he can be certain that it is an artificial life-form as witnessed through the subconscious of the abducted and confused human mind.

The Roswell legacy became the way for the spirits to make man aware of their presence. Yet he did not. So the cover-up emerged. And a new story unfolded many decades later portraying the artificial life-form as the alien that is reptile. Eventually, the reptilian features were perceived as malevolent. Hollywood entered into the scene to have its way by depicting the alien as an evil, grotesque, reptilian life-form that comes to earth to exploit, to invade, to kill, and to destroy human society. This was absolutely absurd! The spirit inside the luminous UFO wasn't a reptile, wasn't a creature. The spirit, who enters into earth's 13th dimension, came not to kill, nor destroy, but to save man from his own imminent demise.

Since 1958 until the year 2000, the Ra Agenda began to disseminate information to specific people. This is not a simple task to do since such a tremendous disparity exists between the awareness of the spirit and the awareness of the human conscious. When the spirit makes contact with the human being, the human conscious cannot deal with the experience. The conscious mind shuts down to prevent the frontal lobe in the left hemisphere from receiving any stimuli; then, the person entered into a catatonic state which is a defense mechanism of the human conscious that is not induced by the spirit of an angel.

Missing time, which prevents someone from remembering the UFO experience, is not induced by the spirit of an angel; it presents itself as a period of amnesia that prevents the conscious mind from remembering the UFO experience. The subconscious from someone who is abducted remains unaffected by the UFO encounter and will follow directions from the spirit of an angel. The angel instills knowledge into the subconscious of the selected subject knowing the information eventually will make its way to the conscious mind. But in order for the angel to accomplish this feat there are two requirements, the spirit needs to follow: first, the angel has to establish the specific gene pool from the human race; second, the artificial life-form is employed to implant a transmitter into the subject to transmit the information into the subconscious.

Now, the human race is born from the mixture of genes that belongs to the aliens from Pluto, from the 10th, from the 11th, and from the 12th Planets and also from the genes of Neanderthal. This difference is detected within the genes of the human being. The angel examines man through the use of the artificial life-form to determine the different types and the percentages of alien in the genes.

In the human being the percentage of alien from the various types ranges from five to fifty-three. Angels sought to establish contact with the human being who falls within the 50 percentile. Five percent of the population on earth belongs to this tiny group. In turn, the combination from the different types of alien in the person's genes is dependent upon the racial make-up which is as follows: The person that comes from a predominantly Anglo-Saxon descent has alien in the genes from the 11th or the 12th Planet mixed with lower percentages of Pluto and Neanderthal; the person that comes from a predominantly African descent has alien in the genes from the Planet Pluto and from Neanderthal mixed with lower percentages from the 11th or 12th Planet; the person that comes predominately from an Indigenous descent (Indian and Asian) has alien in the genes from the Planet Pluto mixed with lower percentages from the 11th or 12th Planet and from Neanderthal, and the person who comes from a predominantly Chinese descent has alien in the genes from the 10th Planet mixed with lower percentages from the 11th or 12th Planet and from Neanderthal

Planet	**Alien**	**Neanderthal**	**Race**
Nibiru (12th)	5 – 53%	5 – 10%	Anglo-Saxon
Eleventh	5 – 53%	5 – 10%	Anglo-Saxon
Tenth	5 – 53%	1 – 5%	Chinese
Pluto	5 – 53%	7.5 – 10%	Indigenous

(fig. 43) Percent of the alien and Neanderthal genes that is present in the human race.

Initially, in 1961, Ra began to examine the human race seeking human beings with Tenth, Eleventh, and Twelve Planet alien genes that measure in the fifty percentile (4.5 % of the population). Ra implanted a transmitter into the selected subject to become able to transmit information to the human subject. Michael and Viracocha sought human beings with genes from Pluto that measure in the 50 percentile. Scarcely, one half of a percent of the human population belongs to this miniscule but highly selected group. Michael and Viracocha began to implant a transmitter into the selected subject starting in 1972.

As a result, five percent of the population from the human race

Gene (50 – 53%)	**Race**	**Population**
Nibiru (12th)	Anglo-Saxon	1.5%
Eleventh	Anglo-Saxon	1.5%
Tenth	Chinese	1.5%
Pluto	Indigenous	.5%
Total percent	Human race	5 %

(fig. 44) Five percent of the human population has 50 – 53% alien genes.

began to receive information that originates from outer space. The information is implanted into the subconscious. Michael and Viracocha choose to implant the information while the subject is asleep, and they induce sleep, in the subject, before the artificial life-form establishes contact; however, Ra chooses to implant the information while the subject is in a trance, and this type of contact from the artificial life-form represents 95 percent of the UFO abduction scenarios.

The human being with less than 50 percent alien in the genes cannot be communicated to by the spirit, but the human who is 50 percent alien in the genes has a subconscious that is receptive to the spirit of the angel. When the artificial life-form establishes contact, the human conscious enters into a trance within seconds into the abduction. While the individual that has Tenth, Eleventh, or Twelve, Planet alien in the genes remains in a trance, Ra transmitted ideas into the right hemisphere, but it takes some 30 years for the conscious memory to receive the information. Once the information is delivered to the conscious mind, it became available to the conscious memory as the process of thought; thus, by the early 90's a new awareness in the consciousness of man began to emerge which is inspired by the recipients to the Ra Agenda. This new consciousness has begun to open the way to the future generation.

Michael and Viracocha will further expedite the Ra Agenda by creating a special generation within the human race – the Ra generation. The Ra Agenda began to remove human sperm from the male whose genes tests 50% alien from Pluto. Michael and Viracocha isolated the Pluto gene and removed the 11th or12th Planet gene from the mixture to leave the Pluto and the Neanderthal genes undisturbed. They implanted the gene mixture into a human ovary to fertilize within the womb of a human female. In such manner, Michael and Viracocha have begun to create the Ra generation within the human race. They began to fertilize the human eggs in 2000 and are scheduled to end in the year twenty-twelve. Within 29 years, by the year 2040, when the age of Aquarius is officially begun, the Ra generation will have grown into mature adults, to choose to lead mankind into the new age.

Consequently, the Ra generation will become less prone to the sexual impulse and genetically will not inherit the need to amass wealth. Wealth of the spirit and beauty in the spirit will be what the Ra generation shall be all about. Man will be placed back on track, on the right path, on the long road to his destiny. The trip will be long, 800 years to be exact, but at the end of the road, man will be left to stand on the same crossroad where he once stood at the start to the Age of Taurus: to choose between his human spirit or his human conscious, between immaterialism or materialism. Man will find himself in the same position the second generation found themselves some 6,000 years ago: the privileged and most gratifying position of establishing spiritual contact with the Progenitor of the Universe.

Therefore, in the coming Age of Aquarius man will be introduced to the age of the enlightenment of the spirit where he will disassociate himself from the illusions that conditioned and enslaved his human soul since the past 2,000 years. In the Age of Pisces, man was introduced to the age of darkness of the spirit. He became like the fish that is taken out of the context of the water (spirit) to become spiritually deprived to live in the un-natural habitat to squirm helplessly while gasping for his last desperate breath. But the coming Age of Aquarius will become for man what the Ancient Mayans predicted all along – the age of the enlightenment of the human spirit. The soul we call man will become transformed like onto living breathing fish that are placed back into the natural habitat of water. His human spirit shall begin to resonate loudly to become vibrant, to be aware, to begin to embrace the idea for universal freedom and to demand social and political reform. Aquarius belongs to the Ra generation, for they, together with the Fifth generation, will help usher the human race into the new and final age for mankind.

UFO Pictures

Courtesy: www.ufocasebook.com

1) Slide Ward—Colorado Ward Sawmill April 1929

This photo was taken by Edward Pline. It remains as one of the earliest UFO photos ever produced: courtesy Hetty Pline.

2) Los Angeles, California, February 25, 1942 (02:25 AM)

A few months after the Japanese attacked Pearl Harbor, residents in Culver City and Santa Monica were the first to be awakened by the sound of sirens and by the sound of anti aircraft fire resulting from the air assault of the Army's 37th Coast Artillery Brigade that was directed at the UFO. The UFO appeared to hang in the air, seemingly undisturbed by the barrage which continued for some 30 minutes, before it proceeded to move slowly away toward Long Beach.

L.A. Times photo

3) Washington D.C. 1952 – UFOs over the White House

For two consecutive weekends UFOs appeared over the restricted airspace over the White House causing major security concerns.

This photo appeared in the Washington POST.

4) Salem Massachusetts July, 16, 1952

This photo was taken by Shel Alpert an AUSCG seaman in the Coast Guard Weather Office at the Salem Coast Guard Station.

5) Sicily Italy December, 10, 1954

6) Edwards Air Force Base, California, Sept, 1957

This photo was taken by a test pilot during a test run of the B-57 twin jet.

Trinidade Island, January, 16, 1958

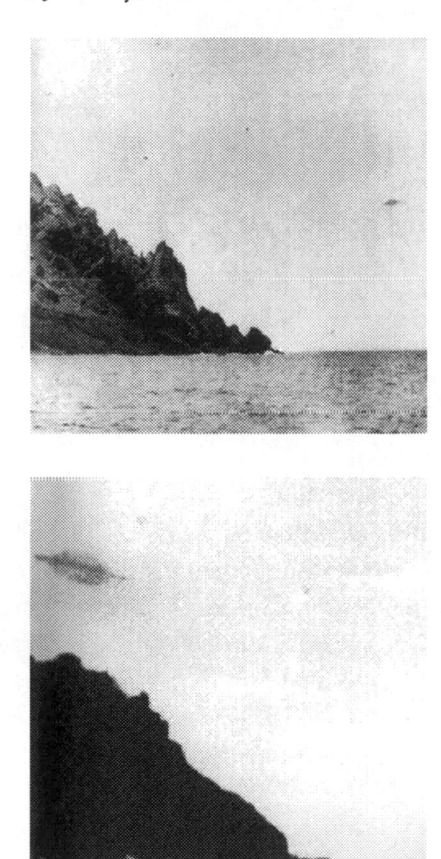

These two photos were taken by a civilian professional photographer named Almiro Barauna. He and the crew were on board the Brazilian Navy Ship "Almirante Saldanha" conducting an oceanographic research study. A UFO suddenly appeared to fly by the island. Everyone on deck, over 50 people including the captain of the ship, witnessed the event. Baruana was able to snap these two historic photos.

Source: Ronald Story's "The Encyclopedia of UFOs" page 366—369

CHAPTER SEVEN

Ezekiel's Vision

From the book of Ezekiel, there emerged an incredible account, an extraordinary encounter that occurs between man and God, a spectacular awe-inspiring vision that stands in the fore-front to the inspiration for the Judeo Christian faith. Ezekiel's vision became frozen in time. The vision allows us to examine through his own words what he observed.

So we examined the biblical evidence, and we searched for the truth, and we conversed with the words of Ezekiel to unravel the vision piece by piece revealing within his description the revelation of God's true glory. To the first impression, the vision appears as a bizarre and illogical description of God, yet Ezekiel describes different components to his vision that if pieced together like a jig-saw puzzle will explain scientifically what he observed, but the story becomes buried under the enormous religious and social taboo of the omnipotent and unquestionable God that we scarcely scratched the surface to reveal the vision's lost and forgotten meaning.

Despite man's hope and his aspirations, the important question remains unanswered! Did Ezekiel experience an awesome and supernatural encounter with the true God, or did he experience an ancient close encounter of the fourth kind with visitors – unknown messengers from outer space? The answer to this elusive question remains a long and forgotten mystery.

But the mystery slowly unraveled itself through the very words of the Prophet Ezekiel who writes he was taken against his will by messengers from outer space and flown away inside a UFO in 593 B.C., for the past 2,500 years since Ezekiel's amazing encounter, angels' have periodically been, through the use of the cyclical age, establishing contact with the human race. In the 21st century, Ra, Michael, and Viracocha have come once again to examine the human race. Although 2,500 years seems to be an enormous length of time, according to the Precession of the Equinoxes, it represents approximate five hours in celestial time, so it appears that just five hours ago, at least according to man's unidirectional way of thinking, the prophet Ezekiel was abducted by Michael near the Chebar River.

In the previous chapter, we discussed the Ra Agenda. Michael, Ra, and Viracocha, began to disseminate knowledge in 1960 to mankind, and the angels first disseminated knowledge to the biblical prophets by 1200 B.C., and the prophets introduced the knowledge into the Holy Bible; however, the information is interpreted into stories that carry in them a hidden meaning. So too did the name for the biblical Lord become synonymous with the names for many gods -- Elohim, El, Isis, the Seven Headed Serpent, Michael, and Ra.

Nevertheless, the book of Ezekiel provides us with the unique opportunity to examine a pivotal time in history when the 12 tribes of Israel – known as the Afro-Asiatic races – were separated through an Agenda of a Snake. The two tribes, Benjamin and Judah, became disunited from the other ten tribes to fall to the lowest level of consciousness when they followed the rituals of the line of Cain. The Seven Headed Serpent was the Lord of the twelve tribes, but after bringing the required level of consciousness to the tribes of Benjamin and Judah, the group no longer chose to remain as Lord for the remaining ten.

After an Agenda transgressed the 12 tribes, the Seven Headed Serpent chose the tribes of Benjamin and Judah to continue an Agenda to create the fourth generation and abandoned the remaining ten tribes. They were left stranded and Michael chose to come to sustain them. As we discovered, the Children of Israel (the tribe of Benjamin) and the House of Israel (the tribe of Judah) were used in the genetic manipulation of alien and human genes to create the Chinese and Girgashite people.

In 597 B.C., the Babylonian King Nebudchanezzar besieged Jerusalem and the sacred temple. Ezekiel and a number of dignitaries were taken as prisoners and transported to a refugee camp located in Tel-Abib. Four years later the refugee Ezekiel experienced his first encounter with the biblical Lord Michael. His vision came complete with an accurate description of a UFO, four artificial life-forms, and a detailed description of what can only be the account off a modern-day lift-off; thus, Ezekiel's ancient close encounter comes replete with the signs of a 21st century UFO abduction stamped all over it!

At first glance, as we read the biblical verses, they convey a bewildering and illogical description of the biblical Lord. So we are brought to believe that God – the Progenitor of the Universe – has appeared to Ezekiel in such a bizarre and bewildering fashion? But what purpose did this confusion serve? Absolutely none! It is logical to assume the almighty and all-powerful God of the Universe didn't appear to Ezekiel at all, for it is impossible for a human to experience physical contact with the true God of the universe because God is an immaterial force and man is a physical animal. It becomes more probable that Ezekiel was approached by the God of man, not by the God of the universe. We contend he was visited by a messenger of God. In this particular instance, it was the angel Michael. Whatever happened on that awe-inspiring day changed Ezekiel's life forever because it transformed him into a messenger between the twelve tribes of Israel and the angel Michael. Now, we introduce Ezekiel's amazing vision.

The biblical narrative begins in the year 593 B.C., in ancient Babylon, near the refugee camp by the river Chebar (Ezekiel 1:4), "And I looked, and, behold, a whirlwind [a UFO] came out of the north, a great cloud and a fire [electromagnetic energy] infolding itself and a brightness was about it... Also out of the midst thereof came the likeness of four living creatures. And this was their appearance; they had the likeness of a man." A rapid moving amber-color bright light approached Ezekiel as he looked to the north. Within an instant, the light had descended upon the earth, and he witnessed four humanoids inside.

The prophet Elisha, too, (2nd Kings 2:11) described a chariot of fire and horses of fire that passed and separated him from the prophet Elijah as they walked side by side by the bank of the Jordan River; then, within an instant, he observed a whirlwind snatch Elijah up into heaven. In both instances, Ezekiel and Elisha describe their observations of a flying object by using the words fire and whirlwind; fire describes the cloud of electromagnetic energy that surrounds the UFO, and whirlwind describes a rapid moving, spinning disc.

Ezekiel chapter1:6 continues, "Each one [corner] had four faces, [facing to the east and west and to the south and north] and each one [creature] had four wings, [at the east and west and at the south and north borders]." Ezekiel compared the four artificial life-forms' faces with the four corners of the UFO and the four creatures non-visualized bodies to the quadruple set of wings which were aligned to the four directions in the compass.

(fig. 45) Creature faces and wings.

He divided the UFO into four parts: four faces, four wings, four feet, four wheels. Then, Ezekiel described the way the UFO functioned by explaining each part separately. Because he never saw a UFO before, Ezekiel thought the UFO was alive. He described it as though it was composed from the bodies of four animals.

In Mexico when Hernando Cortes first arrived, history preserved a similar tale. The Aztec legend foretold of the return of the God Quetzacoatl. When the Spaniards arrived, the Aztec king Moctezuma and his men greeted Cortes and the Conquistadores as returning gods. They viewed the conquistador fully suited in armor and the horse that he was mounted on as one creature – a living god. The Aztecs had never seen a man suited in armor or the horse the conquistador sat on. Likewise, Ezekiel had never seen a UFO before 593 B.C. Both lived by the state of the Michael spirit not by the state of consciousness, so they interpreted what they saw through a higher state of human awareness. The Aztecs and Ezekiel lived by the state of benevolence, and they lived in harmony with the environment and with the forces of nature; however, the Spaniards lived by the state of consciousness, and they immediately made an advantage from the benevolent experience and history recorded the rest of the story, but now we continue with Ezekiel's amazing vision.

Ezekiel chapter1:7, "Their legs were straight [artificial], and the soles [the bottoms] of their feet were like the soles of calves feet. They sparkled like the color of burnished bronze." There were four (not eight) legs, and they were positioned at the east and west and at the south and north corners of the UFO. The legs resemble landing pads and the bottoms were shaped in a manner that is suitable to stabilize the immense weight of the UFO by digging into the ground

(fig. 46) Leg.

Ezekiel chapter1:8, "The hands of a man were under their wings on their four sides; and each of the four had faces and wings." The biblical verse reiterates the direction and the position of the faces and the wings, but now, Ezekiel observed hands directly underneath the set of wings. Although he observed faces and hands, he didn't see any humanoid bodies, and this is because the four humanoids were housed inside the UFO.

(fig. 47) Hands underneath their wings.

We continue (Ezekiel 1:9), "Their wings were joined [connected] one to another; they turned [flapped] not when they went; they went everyone straight forward." The wings of the UFO functioned differently than the wings of a bird because the wings were connected and moved forward and backward and didn't flap, yet every depiction, we see of the wings in Ezekiel's vision or in depictions of gods from the past resembles the wings of a bird. This idea symbolizes the god's ability to fly within the UFO and is never intended to be taken as literal wings of a bird. This error demonstrates how easy it is for man to err when attempting to decipher ancient pictographs or script through the conscious mind. It has led to the erroneous conclusion that the Aztecs and the Mayans practiced the ritual of human sacrifice. However, what should be taken literally in regards to the wings in Ezekiel's vision is the idea of the wings which represent the body of the UFO which housed the artificial life-forms inside.

Ezekiel chapter 1:10, "As for the likeness of their faces, they four had the face of a man [directly in front of Ezekiel's line of sight which faced to the north], and the face of a lion, on the right side [facing to the east]; and they four had the face of an ox on the left side [facing to the west]; they four also had the face of an eagle [facing to the south]." As Ezekiel looked north toward the direction of the landed UFO, he saw directly in front of his line of sight a humanoid face. As he gazed to the right, then to the left and behind the humanoid face, he saw the face of a lion, an ox, and eagle respectively, but these three faces weren't connected to the humanoid face. This is impossible! They weren't faces at all! Aside from the four artificial life-forms' faces that remained stationary within the center of the UFO, Ezekiel saw the east, the west, the south, the north, borders that were rotating in the UFO. He saw three animal faces in the same manner someone can see a face on a tree trunk or a face on a plane by association, so he associated the UFO to the four humanoid faces and described the UFO by comparing it to the body parts of the human being.

Ezekiel chapter 1:11-12, "Thus were their faces: and their wings were stretched upward; two wings of every one were joined one to another [forming a circle], and two covered their bodies. And they went everyone straight forward: Wither the spirit [the UFO] was to go, they [the wings] went; and they turned not when they went." The wings of the UFO were clearly not intended to flap like the wings of a bird; instead, they formed a circle. How else can a total of 16 wings (4 x 4 = 16) that are divided by the four directions connect? A circle becomes the logical geometric pattern for the wings to form; thus, Ezekiel saw the faces and hands of four artificial life-forms inside a reddish glowing circular light. This description fits perfectly with the 21st century description of the UFO which is traditionally described as a glowing circle of light.

Ezekiel chapter 1:13-14, "As for the likeness of the living creatures their appearance was like burning coals of fire, and like the appearance of lamps: it went up and down among the living creatures [effect of electromagnetic energy], and the fire was bright, and out of the fire went forth lightning. And the living creatures ran and returned as the appearance of a flash of lightning [speed of light]." An electromagnetic energy grid within the center of the UFO pulsated and fluctuated and reflected light energy on the artificial life-forms faces and gave them an eerie and glowing appearance. If we are to continue to take Ezekiel's words seriously, we must conclude the UFO traveled back and forth, in front of his eyes, seemingly at the speed of light.

Ezekiel chapter 1:15-16, "Now as I beheld the living creatures, behold one wheel upon the earth by the living creatures, with his four faces. The appearance of the wheels and their work was like unto the color of a beryl [beryllium] and they four had one likeness [standard parts] and the appearance and their work was as it were a wheel in the middle of a wheel [a gyroscope]." Ezekiel saw four wheels touching the ground when the UFO landed, and the wheels resembled each other because they were manufactured as identical parts to the UFO; likewise, when an automobile comes from the manufacturing line, its four wheels look identical, but the wheels to the UFO weren't regular wheels. They constituted a very special substance. Beryllium is a highly resistant and anti-corrosive element that is employed by NASA in its space projects, and it will be hard pressed for anyone at this juncture in the story to deny that this important fact points to a special connection between Ezekiel's vision and visitors from another world.

The highly specialized wheels allowed the UFO to travel on the ground and to move in any direction (Ezekiel 1:17), "When they [the wheels] went, they went upon their four sides: and they turned [rolled] not, when they went." The unique composition of a wheel within a wheel allowed the UFO to turn in any direction as it moved on the ground. The wheels resembled gyroscopes, and they equalized the weight of the UFO as it moved on the ground.

(fig. 48) Wheel within a wheel.

The UFO was an exploratory craft which demonstrated the ability to travel through the air and on the terrain at any given moment. We believe it even possessed the ability to travel underwater. In either case, it moved through the air and on the land with ease (Ezekiel 1:19), "... when the living creatures went, the wheels went by them: and when the living creatures were lifted up from the earth, the wheels were lifted up. Withersoever the spirit was to go, they [the four wheels] went, thither [wherever] was their spirit to go; and the wheels were lifted up over against them: for the spirit [life] of the living creatures was in the wheels." Described in this ancient passage is an account of a phenomenon that the average person in the 21st century observes virtually every single day in his life, for it becomes an accepted fact that under the normal circumstance when an automobile drives away on a road or an airplane flies away in the air the wheels will follow. Although the editor of the verse thought the wheels were alive because they followed the UFO (the living creatures) wherever they went, in reality, the wheels were affixed to the UFO and moved in a direct relationship to it.

If we are to become excited by the incredible information we have just uncovered, we will become ecstatic to read the following verses in Ezekiel 1:22-23, "And the likeness of the firmament [crystal dome] above the heads of the living creatures was as the colour of the terrible crystal, stretched forth over their heads above. And under the firmament [crystal roof] were their wings straight, the one toward the other: everyone had two, which covered on this side, and everyone had two, which covered on that side, their bodies." Wheels that follow the four creatures everywhere they go, a crystal dome that makes direct contact with a set of eight wings that stretch above, a set of eight wings that stretch below to cover the four creatures bodies -- we have disclosed the truth. Ezekiel saw a space craft with gyroscopic instruments and a crystal dome.

(fig. 49) UFO with crystal dome.

As plausible as this evidence has become, it became credible when we defined the word crystal. When used as a natural or a synthetic material, it possesses piezoelectric or semi-conducting properties, and in the field of medicine crystal is implemented as a tool to diagnose disease through the field of ultrasound; furthermore, in the science of electronics crystal revolutionized and facilitated the transmission of audio and video data. Could anything prove itself more amazing than what the subsequent verses reveal?

Ezekiel chapter 1: 25-28, "And there was a voice from the firmament [now a transmitter] that was over their heads, when they stood, and let down their wings. And above the firmament that was over their heads was the likeness of a throne, as the appearance of a sapphire stone and upon the likeness of the throne [the navigator's seat] was the appearance of a man [an angel] above upon it. And I saw as the colour of amber, as the appearance of fire round about within it, from the appearance of his loins [body] even upward, and from the appearance of his loins even downward [an electro magnetic silhouette of an angel], I saw as it were the appearance of fire, and it had brightness round about. As the appearance of the bow that is in the cloud in the day of rain, so was the appearance of the brightness round about. This was the appearance of the likeness of the glory of the Lord. And when I saw it, I fell upon my face, and I heard a voice of one that spake." Incredible! Not at this juncture! The crystal dome possessed the capacity to transmit audio/video data. Not only did Ezekiel hear a voice from above the crystal dome, but also, projected above it, he observed an un-discernable silhouette, an incandescent image that can only be attributed to an angel.

Prophetic wisdom had been communicated to Ezekiel because by his next encounter he renames the beings in the UFO (Ezekiel 10:20), "This is the living creature [the UFO] that I saw under the God of Israel by the river of Chebar; and I knew they were the cheribums." Ezekiel categorized the four winged angel as a cherub. In this particular instance, it was the Cherub Michael that came in a final attempt to prevent the tribes of Benjamin and Judah from transgressing to the level that is necessary for the human conscious to emerge.

Ezekiel chapter 2:1-3 continues, "And he said unto me, Son of man [descendant from Seth], stand upon thy feet, and I will speak unto thee…I send thee to the children of Israel [to the Girgashite people], to a rebellious nation that have rebelled against me: they and their fathers [the Tribe of Judah] have transgressed against me [through the genetic breeding of the line of Seth] even unto this very day." Also, Michael (Ezekiel 3:4), "…said unto me Son of man, go…unto the house of Israel [unto the Rephaim people], and speak with my words unto them." Ezekiel was sent to warn the tribe of Judah and Benjamin of the severity to their transgressions. They had entrapped man's Michael spirit in the 14th and 15th dimensions; upon physical death, man's Michael spirit no longer traveled freely to the fifth dimension. Now, the Michael spirit of a deceased human being remained trapped in limbo while the spirits of El and Isis were free to remain incarnated in the 13th dimension.

Michael came to prevent the remaining 10 tribes from developing the human conscious, but the degeneration in the Afro-Asiatic race reached the limit to which there was no return. Despite this, Michael had a message to deliver to them (Ezekiel 3:11), "... go [Ezekiel], get thee to them of the captivity, unto the children of thy people [the ten tribes] and speak unto them, and tell them, thus saith the Lord God; whether they will hear or whether they will forbear." Michael's job was over. Michael warned the 10 tribes about further degrading their level of consciousness through sexual intercourse with the tribes of Benjamin and Judah. Man became disconnected from Michael. By the end of the Age of Aires, Michael left earth, but now at the end of the age of Pisces (some 2,500 years later), Michael has re-emerged.

Unbeknown to man, his Michael spirit began to degrade as he slowly transformed himself from an herbivore into a carnivore. As he practiced the rituals and sacrifices that are highlighted for him in the book of Exodus, he lowered his awareness in his Michael spirit (ESP) and gained his awareness in consciousness. In the process, he was taught to barbecue meat as a religious ritual, as an offering to God; consequently, by adding meat to the human diet, an Agenda conditioned the human body to rely on protein and lowered man's consciousness to the level of an animal.

We read about the biblical practice of animal sacrifice, but we have no idea what it truly entailed. Most people believe the biblical God in the book of Exodus required man to sacrifice an innocent animal, to mutilate it, to shed its blood on an altar as a reverence to the biblical Lord for man's obedience. There has to be a tale telling sign, a logical reason to explain the ritual of animal sacrifice, so we sought for the answer to discover it within the Old Testament in

(Exodus 38:1), "And he [Moses] made the altar of burnt offering of shittim wood." Moses built a portable altar according to the required dimensions that were given to him by the biblical Lord – which in this occasion is the Seven Headed Serpent (Exodus chapter 38:3), "... he [Moses] made all the vessels [cooking utensils] of the altar, the pots, and the shovels, and the basons, and the fleshhooks, and the firepans: all the vessels thereof made he of brass." A portable sacrificial altar with pots and pans has the appearance of a portable kitchen. Does it not! Well, there is more.

The Seven Headed Serpent instructs Moses to inform the people from the twelve tribes (Leviticus 1:2), "... if any man of you brings an offering unto the Lord, ye shall bring your offering of the cattle [for beef], even of the herd, and of the flock [poultry]." Leviticus chapter1:10-14 goes on to delineate the process for preparing and cooking the meat, "And if his offering be of the flocks, namely of the sheep, or of the goats for a burnt sacrifice [a cooking ritual]; he shall bring it a male without blemish [superior quality]. And he shall kill it on the side of the altar northward before the Lord [direction of the north-star], and the priests, Aaron's sons, shall sprinkle his [the animal's] blood round about upon the altar. And he shall cut [prepare] it into his [cooking size] pieces, with his head and his fat and the priests shall lay them in order on the wood [grill] that is on the fire [charcoal] that is on the altar [barbecue stand]." Should we uphold the erroneous believe the twelve tribes domesticated livestock then mutilated their cattle, lamb, and fowl, by cutting the animals into pieces, burning them, and discarding the burnt pieces to appease the Lord? Preposterous! Man became conditioned through his religious rituals to slowly eat meat and became a carnivore. He was led to believe, because he is supreme over all animals, he could eat them! And it wasn't because of survival! During the third generation, man led two paths: the spiritual herbivorous and the carnal carnivorous path. Man embraced the latter and the book of Genesis provides an answer.

In the book of Genesis lies a lost and forgotten secret, a symbolic tale of jealousy and envy, a forbidden truth that carries far-reaching implications for mankind, and the truth centers itself in the biblical story of Cain and Abel. Genesis chapter 4:1-5, "And Adam knew Eve his wife; and she conceived, and bare Cain, and said, I have gotten a man from the Lord. And she again bare his brother Abel. And Abel was a keeper [domesticator] of sheep, but Cain was a tiller [farmer] of the ground. And in process of time it came to pass, that Cain brought of the fruit [best] of the ground an offering unto the Lord. And Abel, he also brought of the firstlings [best] of his flock and of the fat thereof. And the Lord had respect unto Abel and his offering. But unto Cain and his offering he had not respect."

Why was the biblical Lord dissatisfied with Cain's offering? Did Cain hold back in the quality in his offering or in the sincerity in his spirit? Or was Abel's carnivore diet better than Cain's vegetable? Genesis chapter 4:6-7 continues, "And the Lord [the Seven Headed Serpent] said unto Cain [herbivore], why art thou wroth? And why is thy countenance fallen? If thou doest well [be a carnivore], shall thou not be accepted? And if thou doest not well [be an herbivore], sin [persecution] lieth at the door." Thus, the story of Cain and Abel delineates the moment when the Egyptian and Kenizzite people parted direction to take the Egyptian vegetarian path and the Kenizzite carnivore. However, persecution followed and by the third generation man slowly became a carnivore.

Genesis chapter 4:7 continues, "...And unto thee [you] shall be his [Abel's] desire, and thou [carnivorism] shall rule over him [vegetarianism]. And Cain talked with Abel his brother: and it came to pass, when they were in the field, that Cain rose up against Abel his brother, and slew him (Genesis 4:8). For 1,817 years (the sum of Seth's plus Enos's ages that total two breeding times) the line of Seth remained with the herbivorous diet, but since the end of the age of Taures, through the religious rituals dictated in the book of Exodus and through the transgressions of the Canaanite and later the Kadmonite races, man slowly began to eat meat as an offering to appease the Lord. By the third generation, at the start to the age of Aires, the line of Seth fell into deceit and began to defame man's Michael spirit through the sacrificial ritual of eating meat and by consecrating the blood of an animal.

Thus, by the time of Ezekiel – near the end of the Age of Aires – the 10 tribes had fully developed consciousness, but Ezekiel had not because he remained a vegetarian who lived through the will of his Michael spirit. Ezekiel chapter 4:14, "Then said I, [Ezekiel] Ah Lord GOD! Behold, my soul hath not been polluted; for from my youth up even till now have I not eaten of that which dieth of itself [meat], or is torn in pieces; neither came there abominable flesh into my mouth."

Michael implanted information into Ezekiel's subconscious to inform him about the future restoration of the temple of Jerusalem that was to occur at the beginning of the Age of Aquarius, but contrary to man's believe, the temple isn't going to be restored in modern day Jerusalem but in the United States of America. Where is this temple to be built? Well, it depends on the meaning we give to the word. By definition, a temple is a building of worship, but a building of worship stands meaningless without the congregation to fill it. The new temple of Jerusalem represents not the hallowed-out dried bones that filled the old temple – the Levite people, but the meat and flesh that covers the bones of a new people – the fifth generation. They are a mixture of the oppressed and the oppressor, a new breed that proliferated around the world. The fifth generation is the result of almost 500 years of Anglo-Saxon dominance over the descendants of Seth. Ironically, the letters USA are found within the very center of the name of Jer<u>usa</u>lem to mark the place where the parents and the grandparents of the fifth generation started a change in 2008. This change continues to spread throughout the globe, a wave of a newer consciousness that will demand change throughout the world. One thing we can be certain! The new temple of Jerusalem isn't a building to be found anywhere on earth, but as a new breed of people, as a new generation with a higher level of awareness, the new temple of Jerusalem has proliferated everywhere, on every single geographic region that exists on planet earth.

Thus, Ezekiel's vision of the valley of dry bones brings hope for the restoration of man's human spirit (Ezekiel 37:1-3), "The hand of the Lord was upon me, and carried me out in the spirit of the Lord, and set me down in the midst of the valley which was full of bones.

And caused me to pass by them round about: and, behold, there were very many in the open valley; and, lo, they were very dry. And he [Michael] said unto me, Son of man can these bones [the human race] live [have Michael spirit]. And I answered, O Lord God thou knowest." What follows is a symbolic portrayal of the restoration of the temple "people" of Jerusalem (Ezekiel 37: 9-11), " Then said he unto me, prophesy unto the wind, prophesy, son of man, and say to the wind, Thus saith the Lord God; come from the four winds, O, breath, and breathe upon these slain, that they may live. So I prophesied, as he commanded me, and the breath came into them, and they lived, and stood up upon their feet, an exceeding great army. Then he said unto me, Son of man, these bones are the whole house of Israel [the five races in the human family]: behold they say, our bones are dry [man's Michael spirit is dead] and our hope is lost: we are cut off for our parts [man is cut off from his Michael spirit].

So man's Michael spirit remains slain. His slain bones represent the spiritual death of the human race. Michael will fulfill the will of Elohim and will return with Ra and Viracocha at the end of Pisces to restore man's Michael spirit to its rightful place. Ezekiel chapter 37:12-14, "Therefore prophesy [foretell the future] and say unto them [the human family – Indigenous, Afro-Asiatic, Asian, Chinese, Anglo-Saxon races], Thus saith the Lord God [Michael]; Behold, O my people, I will open your graves [free you from reincarnation], and cause you to come up out of your graves, and bring you into the land of Israel [the land of the infinite consciousness]. And ye shall know that I am the Lord, when I have opened your graves, O my people, and brought you up out of your graves. And shall put my spirit [eternal] in you, and ye shall live [through the will of the Michael spirit], and I shall place you in your own land [the anatomical location for man's Michael spirit – the right hemisphere of the human brain]."

Ezekiel's vision by the river Chebar and in the valley of dry bones brings a message of hope for the human race. According to Ezekiel, the heavenly messengers have a destiny to fulfill for the future of man. In Ezekiel's first encounter with Michael, he is taken aboard the UFO to become imparted with prophetic wisdom. What follows is the conclusion to this most incredible encounter. One fact becomes perfectly clear. The vision has the makings of a classic UFO abduction experience!

Ezekiel chapter 3:12-14, "Then the spirit took me up [he is taken on board], and I heard behind me a voice of a great rushing... [the force of propulsion]. I heard also the noise of the wings of the living creatures that touched one another [as the UFO prepares for a take-off], and the noise of the wheels over against them [as they are lifted up from the ground], and a voice of a great rushing [from the acceleration]. So the spirit lifted me up, and took me away..." There can be no mistake that Ezekiel describes a departure that becomes reminiscent of an airplane as it departs from a runway. The sound from the UFO's wings and from the wheels as it prepares for a take-off followed by the sound of a tremendous force of propulsive energy that is necessary to lift the UFO into the air becomes unmistakable, and it cannot be attributed to coincidence. What follows next is even more amazing, for Ezekiel describes not just a take-off, but also a 21st century UFO abduction scenario.

Ezekiel chapter 3:14 continues, "...and I went in bitterness, in the heat of my spirit [against his will]; but the hand of the Lord [the force of gravity] was strong upon me [in the pit of his stomach]. Then I came to them of the captivity at Tel-abib that dwelt by the river of Chebar, and I sat where they sat, and remained there astonished among them seven days." Ezekiel's vision of the four living creatures becomes eerily similar to the Hill's and Travis Walton's (a famous UFO abduction case from 1975) experiences; all three experiences share a number of common similarities. Both accounts describe a glowing UFO. The hills and Travis Walton find themselves aboard a spacecraft literally taken against their free will. They come into contact with strange humanoids. The beings fly them away inside the crafts to an undisclosed location. Later, the Hill's and Walton are brought back to the vicinity where they were abducted; furthermore, the period of shock which affected the Hill's and Walton's level of awareness is consistent with the phenomenon called missing time.

In summary, Ezekiel's vision became Michael's message to man in the 21st century. Michael is preparing man for his final destiny by sending messengers to aid the human race through the coming Age of Aquarius.

CHAPTER EIGHT

The Mayan and the Biblical Apocalypse

A long time ago the Calendar Round, the Long Count, and the book of *the Revelation of Saint John* complimented one another. All three shared in the same message: the message of hope coupled by the despair, of triumph amid the defeat. The Calendar Round, the *Revelation*, and the Long Count, foretold of a future time when the human race will once more become transformed into another generation: through the passage of time, through the passage of the fourth Mayan age. The Mayan Calendar and *the Revelation* share a mutual interest in the destiny of man; bequeathed to him by Viracocha and by Elohim, they alert man as to the approaching end time. The Calendar Round was used by the Kenite people about 4,000 years ago to start the count for the 21.60 centuries in the cyclical Age of Aires. The Tzolkin and the Haab were two of the three centuries that remained in the Age of Aires, and they would lead man into the final century and through the continuous path in time directly into the Long Count calendar to start the Age of Pisces. *The Revelation* was written at the dawn of the Common Era some 1,900 years ago, and like the Long Count it too predicted the end of the world.

The Mayan calendar informed man about the arrival of the fifth and final Mayan Age, and the *Revelation* informed man about the arrival of the fifth and final generation. Both foretold the finale to the Age of Pisces as the start to the final age and as the beginning to the final generation. The approaching end time (as we will learn in the next chapter) refers to the conclusion of the cyclical world of consciousness which will end in approximately 1,200 years.

Now, the Long Count focused on the new age while the book of *the Revelation* focused on the new generation, and while the Long Count remains a complete misunderstood and unsolved mystery, *the*

Revelation of Saint John seemingly does not, for it becomes available to the western world through the book of books – the Bible. So we will begin our search into the end time through *the Revelation* which was inspired by the Archangel Elohim and was written by John the Baptist while he lived in unknown exile in the Greek island of Patmos.

Once more (as in the book of Ezekiel) we are confronted by verses that can only describe a 21st century UFO encounter (Revelation 4:2), "And immediately I [John] was in the spirit [inside the UFO]: and, behold, a throne was set in heaven, and one sat on the throne. And he that sat was to look upon as a jasper and a sardine stone: and there was a rainbow round about the throne in sight like unto an emerald."

One more instance where we find the mention of an angel, but this time it is written within the book of *the Revelation,* and like Ezekiel, John too saw the form of an angel as it transformed from the incorporeal form of the first dimension into the corporeal form of earth's 13th dimension – an incandescent light show that displayed the visible color spectrum through a brilliant electromagnetic energy source.

John continues (Revelation 4:4-5), "…I saw four and twenty elders [aliens], sitting, clothed in white raiment [electromagnetic silhouettes]; and they had on their heads crowns of gold [transformers]. And out of the throne proceeded lightnings and thunderings and voices."

John observed from the UFO's crystal dome the projected audio/video image of an angel sitting on the navigational chair inside; in the same manner, Ezekiel observed above the crystal dome the projected audio/video image of a cherub angel sitting on the navigational chair of the UFO. In both instances, the parallels between the two stories are remarkably similar, for not only are the two occupants inside the UFOs described as sitting on chairs that look like a throne, but also, John and Ezekiel see the angels images projected through a dome which is composed from crystal, and as the fields of medical science and innovational technology have clearly demonstrated in this 21st century filled with inventions, the mineral crystal possesses the ability to transmit audio/video data. Without further delay, we will conclude that some form of movie was projected from the crystal dome and shown to John when he was taken into the UFO.

What other explanation can there be for the verses that follow (Revelation chapter 4:6), "And before the throne was a sea of glass like unto crystal [the image of a throne is projected from the crystal dome]: and in the midst of the throne, and round about the throne [the interior circumference of the UFO], were four beasts [at the north, east, south, and west corners] full of eyes [that protected the throne] before (on front) and behind."

John described the interior surface of the UFO by associating the four directions of the compass to the UFO's four borders. To John's eyes, the UFO's four borders resembled the four faces of animals. The presumed eyes of the animals spread out from each of the four faces to become the internal circumference of the UFO. John states (Revelation chapter 4:7), "And the first beast was like a lion, and the second beast like a calf, and the third beast had the face as a man, and the fourth beast was like a flying eagle."

With the exception of the face of an ox (Ezekiel 1:10) and the face of a calf (Revelation 3:7), the other three faces that are described in the biblical verses are identical. We believe that John and Ezekiel used the four faces to describe the north, east, south, and west borders of the UFO. The four beasts that John described were full of eyes. The eyes represent the UFO's body; thus, each of the four beasts body (each side of the UFO) connected to each of the four faces (each border) to produce the circumference of the UFO. The crystal dome sat directly above. However, John's description alludes as to a different type of UFO then the UFO that Ezekiel saw (Revelation 4:8), "And the four beasts had each of them six wings about him."

The UFO that comes with six wings signifies the seraph angel, and Ezekiel described a UFO that comes with four wings which belongs to the cherub angel; thus, by introducing the seraph angel into the apocalypse, John brings a lost unknown meaning to the Revelation. If we recall, after the fall of the Seraphim rank, one third of the 16th and one third of the 17th Planet angels remained loyal to the mandate of the Seven Heavens. John saw a 17th Planet un-fallen Seraph Angel and twenty-four aliens. They came to instruct him about the coming events to the Age of Pisces, about the fifth generation, and about the end to the fifth Mayan Age of Aquarius.

We continue as John sees (Revelation chapter 5:1), "…in the right hand of him that sat on the throne a book written within and on the backside, sealed with seven seals." The seraph angel sitting on the throne proclaimed if someone worthy could come forward to open the seals. When the worthy one steps forward and opens the first seal (Revelation 6:2), "I [John] saw, and behold a white horse [the Anglo-Saxon races]: and he that sat on him had a bow [superior weaponry]; and a crown [the human conscious] was given unto him; and he went forth conquering, and to conquer."

If the Anglo-Saxon races do represent the white horse, the opening of the first seal will become consistent with the last third of the Age of Pisces which according to the Long count (2x720) started in 1440 of the Common Era. History teaches us that different groups of Anglo-Saxons left their respective countries in Europe for the hope of establishing colonies in the New World. Aside from skipping China, they invaded the world at the end of the 15th century, and they did so by using the human conscious to create superior weapons of war. Tragically, the Indigenous races were controlled by the human conscious through the use of slavery.

Will man ever accept the truth about the Mayan people! Throughout 1,440 years (two-thirds of the Age of Pisces), the Mayan culture lived isolated from the rest of the world. They anticipated the moment when the European settlers would invade the New World, and the long awaited prophecies from the Long Count would become fulfilled. They waited for the arrival of Michael, Ra, and Viracocha, for it is written in the Long Count that they would return at the end of the 15th century to remove the Mayan people before the prophesized return of the sons of the fallen angels – the Anglo-Saxon whose very name implies the genetic link to Isaac who was an incarnated fallen angel. Thus, the Anglo-Saxon invasion of the New World is foretold not just in the Revelation but also in the Long Count. This prophecy was carried over into the Aztec and Inca legends after the Mayans left earth and is the sole reason why the Aztecs and the Incas at the end of the 15th century perceived the arriving Conquistadores as returning gods,

However, no match stood the human spirit for the descendants of the third generation to withstand the greed, the deceit, and the perversion from the human conscious, so they were physically and spiritually enslaved. The identity, the inherent nature of these peaceful people was removed and became replaced with the portrayal of a spiritless and savage one. Their sacred writings were burned. Their scientific and sophisticated cultures were usurped before their very eyes and then desecrated before them and replaced with mundane and simplistic ones.

So man has created the problems he encounters today! Through his apathy, his ignorance, and above all his egocentric selfishness -- he has created the economic, social, and political barriers that challenge the world today. Will man ever awaken himself from his mental stupor? Will he ever discover the truth? Only when the prince's of light intervene for man's behalf! Only when he acknowledges the heavenly messengers -- the angels inside the UFO who are here to fulfill the will of the Progenitor of the Universe – will man free himself from his spiritual bondage. If not, he will be destined to wait until the biblical day of harvest when his human conscious shall be left to decide his final outcome. Needless to say, the last 700 years (the last 1/3 of the Age of Pisces) has spread the human conscious throughout the Indigenous races through sexual intercourse between the Anglo-Saxon and the Indigenous races.

Today the human conscious is manifest in every human being and is seemingly running out of control thriving on sexual stimuli and on physical instincts, but as man is presently finding out, 21st century human consciousness is being transformed into a new level of awareness.

Now, the second seal is open (Revelation 6:4), "And there went out another horse that was red [the Chinese nation]: and power [money] was given to him that sat thereon to take peace from the earth, and that they [the world] should kill one another: and there was given unto him a great sword [North Korea]." Since July 2009, the human race remains poised since the symbolic opening of the second seal. Nations around the world wait with nervous anticipation for a resolution to the global economic crises that faces the world while China remains unscathed, uninterrupted by the current global economic turmoil. North Korea remains defiant hiding behind the scenes of a possible Chinese and North Korean connection.

The third seal is opened (Revelation 6:5-6), "And I beheld, and lo a black horse [the fifth generation]; and he that sat on him had a pair of balances [fairness and equality] in his hand. And I heard a voice in the midst of the four beasts say, A measure of wheat [food] for a penny, and three measures of barley [drink] for a penny; and see thou hurt not the oil [the well being] and the wine [the spirit]." Those verses speak to each of us who are seeing the fifth generation unfold before our eyes. The difference of some ten million less votes in the presidential election in the United States in 2004 as compared to the one that occurred in 2008 reflects this new view of the fifth generation. This transformation in human consciousness began to manifest in the U.S. in 2008 when the first successful African-American presidential candidate was elected into office. Symbolically, President Barak Obama stands not only as the 44th president of the U.S.A, but also as the voice from the fifth generation, for he literally comes from the mixture of the oppressed and the oppressor.

In June in the year 2009, the intensity in the transformation in human consciousness extended from the United States to enter into the Iranian society but to a higher and nobler degree. Valiant young women and young men chose to risk their limbs and their lives demanding from the Iranian government and from the rest of the world a new beginning. This new consciousness has begun to spread throughout the Middle Eastern nations, and it belongs to the remnants of the fourth generation – the 20 to 30 year old people. They are the parents of the children from the fifth generation. Within the next forty-two years, the first influx of the fifth generation will start to bloom while the final outflow of the fourth generation will begin to wilt and to fade and to experience the biblical death of the generations before it by blending into the genetic make-up of every human being. Within the next 250 years, the five families of the human race will assimilate into the fifth generation.

Now, the fourth seal is open (Revelation 6:8), "And I looked, and behold a pale horse [disease] and his name that sat on him was Death, and Hell [the up-rise in the Middle East] followed with him. And power was given unto them [the rulers] over the fourth part of the earth [the Middle East] to kill with sword and with hunger and with death, and with the beasts of the earth [modern machines of war]."

In the 21st century, man continues to be the contributor to his own demise. In the United States alone, heart disease and cancer account for more than 50 percent of the annual death toll. These two diseases are caused by the unnatural life-style in which man is conditioned to live under. Disease will continue to run rampant unless man reverts to the natural and simple life-style of the Mayan people who lived, and were protected, by the eternal laws of nature.

Tunisia: December, 17, 2010, a vegetable-vendor Mohamed Bouazizi is approached by the authorities for not having a license. The authorities confiscate his produce, and purportedly one of the officers slaps Bouazizi in the face. Shamed and left without his only means to survive, the 26 year-old became despondent. That same day, outside of the governor's office, he drenches himself in gasoline and attempts to kill himself by igniting his body on fire. Although Mohamed Bouazizi died 17 days later, his act of self immolation turned him into an instant martyr, and on that same day a series of peaceful protests began to ring throughout Tunisia.

Tunisia: January 14, 2011, after 28 days of protests that left approximately 300 dead and 700 injured protesters, President Zine El Abidine Ben Ali resigned from his 23 year rule of the Tunisian government. This quick victory by the enraged Tunisian population produced a spark that traveled to Tahrir Square in Cairo Egypt and rekindled itself 11 days later.

Egypt: January 25, 2011, Inspired by the success of the protesters in the Tunisian revolt, thousands of Egyptians march out into the streets to protest against widespread poverty, unemployment, and government corruption. They demand the ousting of President Hosni Mubarak who has ruled Egypt for approximately 30 years.

Eighteen days of bloody protests ensues that left approximately 300 dead and over 1,000 injured. Then, President Mubarak feeling the pressure from the protestors and from the international community resigns from office on February, 11, 2011. For the world, this stunning victory became the beginning, the tip of the ice-berg, for it would set of a series of spontaneous revolutions that began to spread throughout the Middle East.

Heart disease, cancer, and the resistant strains in the flu and the revolutions in the Middle East will open the fourth seal to start the 21st century of the Age of Pisces (2111 in the Calendar Round) which coexists with the start of the 21st century of the Common Era (2011 in the Gregorian calendar). The Age of Pisces and the Age of Aquarius will mesh together until Pisces ends and Aquarius begins. Technically speaking, this is supposed to occur at the end of the 60 years that remain for the 21st century of the cyclical Age of Pisces (21.60 – 21.0 = 60 years). The Mayan calendar foretells the 21st century in the Gregorian calendar as a time of impending turmoil and political upheaval. It marks a time in the 21st century of the Age of Pisces exactly 25, 920 years since the Ancient Egyptian people were created through the breeding ritual. Now, in the year 2011 of the Common Era, the modern Egyptian people will have reached the great anniversary of the ancient Egyptian people's birth. The complete cycle in Precession (12 x 2,160 = 25,920 years) is about to be fulfilled, and the human race is about to reach a new level of conscious awareness.

This new awareness, this complete refusal by young people to accept things as they are and to demand social and political reform is a product of the 21st century thought and is described in Revelation 6:8 as Hell on earth. Hell began in Tunisia at the end of the year 2010 before the 21st century in the Calendar Round begins. The 21st century in the Calendar Round is expressed in the Gregorian calendar through code as the number 111; the number 100 represents the 21st century; the number 11 represents the eleventh year -- or 2011. If 2011 is subtracted from 2111, the difference of the number 100 marks the official start of the 21st century for mankind.

21st century C.R. –	2111- 2000 = 111
21st century Gregorian	
Code 111 – 11th year	111- 11 = 100
Start 21st century	100

(fig. 50).

The Calendar Round allows for everyone who is born in the 20th century to add the last two digits from the year they are born to the age they are going to be in the year 2011 and arrive at the exact sum of 111.

Year of birth + age in 2011 =	111
Example: 1910 + 101 = 10 + 101 =	111= 21st century

(fig. 51) Hidden code in the calendar for anyone born in 1900 -1999.

Also, the Calendar Round allows for everyone (children at this point) who is born in the 21st century to add the last two digits from the year they are born to the age they are going to be in the year 2011 and arrive at the exact sum of 11.

Year of birth + age in 2011 =	11
Example: 2001 + 10 = 1 + 10 =	11= 1st century

(fig. 52) Hidden code in the calendar for anyone born in 2000 - 2099.

The formula that allows for these two numbers to occur was understood by the Mayan people, for they incorporated it in the Calendar Round. They divided the 2,160 years in the Age of Pisces by 100 to designate 21.60 centuries. They began to count time for Pisces since the year Jesus was born in 11 B.C., eleven years before the Age of Pisces begins. The second century began in 111 C.E. Each century increases until the 21st century 2011 is reached. The

Mayans used the zero to represent the final 49 years (0.49 centuries) that remain in the Age of Pisces. As we demonstrated in chapter six, 20 years are to be deducted from the remaining 49 years to compensate for the Calendar Round (11 yrs.) and the Long Count (9 yrs.); this brings the remaining count for the Age of Pisces to 29. Thus, mankind has 29 years left in the 21st century before it enters into the first century of the fifth and final Mayan Age of Aquarius in the year 2040 of the Common Era.

The codes 111 and 11 become sacred numbers of the Mayan calendar; the number 111 signifies the beginning to the end of the fourth Mayan Age of Pisces; the number 11 signifies the beginning of the fifth and final Age of Aquarius. On the sunset of September 23, 2011 (autumnal equinox) mankind will leave the 20th century and officially enter into the 21st and final century for Pisces. Then, on the sunset of March 20, 2012 (the vernal equinox), two great events will be commemorated: it will be exactly 2,111 years since the birth of Jesus, and a Great Age of 25,920 yrs will elapse to coincide with the time the ancient Egyptian people were created. On the sunset of September 23, 2040 (autumnal equinox) man will leave the 21st century of the Common Era and enter into the first century of the fifth Mayan Age of Aquarius.

Date	Event
9-23-2011 (autumnal equinox)	Mayan 21st century will begin (4th seal is opened)
3-20-2012 (vernal equinox)	25,920 yrs. (1 Great Cycle) since ancient Egyptians were created and 2,111 yrs since Jesus was born
9-23-2040 (autumnal equinox)	End of 21st century in Pisces: start of 1st century in Aquarius

(fig. 53)

Ancient man counted a complete day as a cycle that began from the first evening and ended on the first morning as opposed to modern man who counts a complete day as a cycle that begins on the first morning and ends on the first evening. The Bible confirms this matter quite clearly (Genesis 1:3-5), "And God said, Let there be light. And God saw the light, that it was good: and God divided the light from the darkness. And God called the light Day, and the darkness he called Night. And the evening and the morning were the first day." Thus, a celestial day begins on the first evening, and an earthly day begins on the first morning.

If we examine dates of events that occur within the last 11 years in the 21st century and apply to them the knowledge we have attained of the Calendar Round, we will discover a code hidden within the Gregorian calendar which the Mayans understood so well. The Egyptian revolt began on the numerical date of 01-25-2011; if the number that corresponds to the month of January stands alone (to represent the 21st century) while the remaining digits are added together (to represent the 11th year) the result will be 100+2+5+2+0+1+1=111. This code represents the start to the 21st century for the Age of Aires as seen 2,000 years into the past,

Aires B.C. (past)		Pisces C.E. (present)	
CENTURY	**CALENDAR ROUND**	**GREGORIAN**	**CENTURY**
0 =	2160 - 1 00 =	11 + 100	= 1st
21st =	**2060 - 100 =**	**111 + 100**	**= 2nd**
20th =	1960 - 1 00 =	211 + 100	= 3rd

(fig. 54)

but most importantly it reflects the second century for the Age of Aires as seen 2000 years into the future Age of Pisces in the 21st century which begins on September 23, 2011

Aires B.C. (past)		Pisces C.E. (present)	
CENTURY	**CALENDAR ROUND**	**GREGORIAN**	**CENTURY**
3rd Tzolkin =	260 - 100 =	1911 + 100	= 20th
2nd =	**160 - 100 =**	**2011 + 100**	**= 21st**
1st =	60 - 49 =	2111 + 49	= 0

(fig. 55).

We continue with the resignation of President Mubarak who resigned on 02-11-2011; this date literally signifies the opening of the fourth seal in the book of revelation which is first measured from the 3rd century of Pisces as seen 1800 years into the past or 2000-211=1789 B.C.

Aires B.C. (past)		Pisces C.E. (present)
CENTURY	CALENDAR ROUND	GREGORIAN CENTURY
21st =	2060 - 100 =	111 + 100 = 2nd
20th = (1789)	**1960 - 100 =**	**211 + 100 = 3rd**
19th =	1860 - 100 =	311 + 100 = 4th

(fig. 56)

This step also reflects the 3rd century for Aires as well, as seen 1800 years into the future or 1800+211=2011 C.E.,

Aires B.C. (past)		Pisces C.E. (present)
CENTURY	CALENDAR ROUND	GREGORIAN CENTURY
4th Haab =	160 - 100 =	1811 + 100 = 19th
3rd Tzolkin =	**260 - 100 =**	**1911 + 100 = 20th (2011)**
2nd =	160 - 100 =	2011 + 100 = 21st

(fig. 57)

and it can be separated, as well as the other codes, as one for the past and the other for the future. The number 211 indicates a time 1800 years into the past (1800-211) = 1589 B.C., but the number 211 also indicates the 20thst century of the Common Era 1800 years into the future (1800+211) = 2011.

Past ←	Present →	Future
1589 B.C.	211C.E.	2011C.E.

(fig. 58).

To reveal the rich symbolism behind the resignation of President Mubarak which occurred exactly on the date 02-11-2011, the code for the past century 211 becomes subtracted from the present century of 2111 in the Calendar Round to derive at the year 1900 which represents the 20th century for the present Age of Pisces. Then, the second code for the present century 2011 becomes subtracted from 2111 in the calendar Round to derive at the year 100 which represents the first century for the Age of Aquarius.

Mayan 21st century - 3rd century Gregorian calendar =	2111 - 211 = 1900 (20th century Pisces)
Mayan 21st century - 21st century Gregorian calendar =	2111- 2011 = 100 (1st century Aquarius)

(fig. 59)

Thus, the code 111 represents the start of the 21st century for Pisces; the code 211 represents the end of the 20th century for Pisces, and the code 11 represents the start of the 1st century for the new Age of Aquarius.

The symbolism that lies behind the code for people who are born in the 20th century (111) and for people who are born in the 21st century (11) is remarkable. The young people from Egypt who are born from 1989 to 2000 belong to the last remnant of the 20th century (111) and they symbolically began the up-rise on 01-25-2011 or 111. The number 111 coincides with the completion (in the 21st century 25,920 years later) of the great cycle in Precession of the Age of Pisces, a time when the descendants from the line of Seth (the Arabic and Native American people) will experience the rebirth in the awareness of the human conscious. When President Mubarak resigned on 02-11-2011, he conceded to the demands of the 111 generation who was bringing freedom to the 11 generation -- the children born since the year 2000. They will have the new start in the new Age of Aquarius.

Furthermore, the historic event that became forever edged in modern history as September 11 represents the Mayan year 911 which can indicate a time 400 years into the past (911-400) =511 C.E., or 400 years into the present (911+400) = 1311 C.E.

Past ←	**Present →**	**Future**
389 B.C.	911 C.E.	1349 C.E.

(fig. 60)

The year 1311 indicates the 14th century – a time when Islam became a major religion. However, in the 21st century, the code 911 indicates not Islam, but the radical extremist groups like Al Qaeda. These groups interpret the Koran and the Islamic faith through the radical movement that seeks reform through the infliction of deadly force and aggression.

The older religion Christianity also experienced the same aberration in thought through the cults that began in the decade of the 1970. On November 18 1978, Rev. Jim Jones, the spiritual leader for the Peoples Temple in northwestern Guyana, became responsible for the death of 918 people who were inside the settlement. All but two died by cyanide poisoning. Ironically, the mass poisoning at the Peoples Temple, as a non-natural catastrophe, remained the largest single loss of civilian life in American history until the events of September eleventh. On 911 the act from the Islamic extremist group Al Qaeda and the Christian cult the Peoples Temple met as one to produce the two deadliest non-natural disasters in American history. This aberration of thought culminated in the 21st century with the allegations of child molestation that surfaced against clergy from the diocese of the Catholic Church, to challenge the fate of Catholicism forever. The younger religion Islam, through the natural course of time, is experiencing this same transformation.

Suffice it to say, The Calendar Round, NATO, and the USA may already have determined the fate for Al Qaeda. On 05-01-2011 President Barak Obama in a televised speech to the American people announced the capture and the death of Osama Bin Laden the alleged leader and mastermind behind the 911 terror plot that killed some 3,000 innocent people in the bombing of the twin towers in New York in 2001. Although President Obama addressed the nation on the evening of May 1st, the top secret mission was conducted in the early morning hours on 05-02-2011.

Again, we employ the Calendar Round to determine the present. The single digits from the month, day, and century are added together (5+2+2+0 = 9) and combined with the 11th year to form the numerical code 911. Is it a coincidence that Osama Bin Laden is killed on a date that points to the events of 911? If it is, what are the odds? And what odds can there be for the same numbers to repeat themselves. Two days before Bin Laden's death. Saif Al-Arab Gaddafi (son of Muammar) was killed by NATO air-strikes when an estimated three missiles hit his home in Libya on 04-30-2011. Again we can add the corresponding digits (4+3+0+2 = 9) and combine the 9 with the 11th year to derive at 911.

Event	**Date**	**Code**
Ghaddafi	04+3+0+2+0 (11)= 9 (11)	911
Bin Laden	05+02+2+0 (11) = 9 (11)	911

(fig. 61)

Two Islamic extremists were killed just two days apart, and the date of their deaths point to the end of their lives which in the Calendar Round points to 911 which points to the end of Al Qaeda. But if Al Qaeda is going to end when is it? Well, the numerical date for the event that destroyed the twin towers is 09-11-2001; to determine the future, 911 is added into 2001 to derive at the future date of 2912 which indicates a time in the future when an event of the catastrophic proportions of 911 will occur. But to determine the present, each digit from the month and from the days is added together (9+1+1= 11). Eleven is added to the year 2001 to derive at the year 2012; thus it is possible, in the year 2012, for an event associated with the end of Al Qaeda to occur. The event that can end the severely crippled Al Qaeda net-work is already in progress as the

Arab spring. These noble and courageous young women and men are seeking freedom and reform. They are not embracing tyranny and oppression. They are fighting for a new cause, for a new era which they call freedom. They are the unlikely recipients to the Al Qaeda network which offers them the old 20th century way of life while they are seeking the new 21st century. They have become the adherents to their own children's -- the fifth generation's -- destiny. Therefore, let peace ring through the Middle East. Let hope spring from the people of these Arab nations that have rebelled against the regimes that dictate and control their right for freedom. One question remains before the aftermath that began just before the Mayan 21st century in 2011. How many more Arab nations will become liberated in the year 2011? Perhaps, fate, through the Mayan calendar, through NATO and through the USA coalition forces, will determine this number to be the sacred number eleven which will combine with the 29 years remaining to begin the first century for the new Age of Aquarius.

The ability to determine, through each Mayan century, present events that occurred years ago from the past or that will occur years later in the future is determined as the difference between earthly and celestial time. This difference amounts to 10,000 years or one celestial day. Thus, the centuries from the Calendar Round are literally the minutes, and the five ages from the long Count are the hour-hands that are ticking at specific intervals of time etched within the celestial day in consciousness that is frozen within the clock, the monument, called the Mayan calendar.

We have brought forth the mind-set that allows us to understand events that are destined to occur within this final 21st century. Let us continue to review the numerical evidence. On January 12, 2010 a catastrophic 7.9 earthquake struck the country of Haiti leveling the capital and killing an estimated 240,000 people. The Haiti earthquake as a localized event surpassed the earthquake and deadly tsunami in Indonesia which killed an estimated 226,000 people in dozens of countries in 2004. The number 1 (because it comes first) will be understood to represent the 21st century; the next two digits will represent the 12th year. If 112 is added to the year 2010, the Mayan year of 2122 results. If the present year of 2011 is subtracted from the Mayan year 2122, the resulting number becomes the code for the 21st century 111. The Haiti earthquake occurred on 2010 which is one year before the year 2011 when the 21st century for the Age of Pisces is scheduled to begin. This slight difference in the value of one year does not affect the numerical computation for the code 111.

Month and day + year	112 + 2010 =	2122
2122 - Mayan 21st century	2122 - 2111 =	111

(fig. 62) Haiti Earthquake.

The earthquake in Haiti forewarns man as to the future calamities that will befall him in the new 21st century.

Approximately 13 months after the earthquake in Haiti occurred and one month in exact since the revolt ended in Egypt, the island of Japan suffered a 9.0 earthquake and a devastating tsunami followed leaving some 800 people dead, hundreds injured. Sadly, the disaster crippled six nuclear reactors. Although the exact details as to the severity of the radiation contamination may never be known, it is confirmed two reactors have leaked out radiation into the ocean and into the surrounding environment. The tragedy in Japan occurred on the numerical date of 03-11-2011, and the code 311 represents a catastrophe that occurred in 1589 B.C. (determined by subtracting 311 from 1900), and it repeated in the 20th century in 1949 (360+1900=2260-311=1949) through the phenomenon called celestial time.

Aires	**Pisces**	**Pisces**
1589 B.C. =	1900 cyclical years - 311 C.E. =	4th C.E.
360 B.C.+ 1900 cyclical years =	2260 - 311 C.E. =	1949 C.E.

(fig. 63).

If 311 is added to the year 2011, the sum is 2322; if 2111 is subtracted from 2322, the difference is 211, and the code 211 symbolizes the opening of the fourth seal; therefore, the meltdown of the six nuclear reactors in Japan is intricately connected to the pale horse in the opening of the fourth seal.

Aires B.C. (past)		Pisces C.E. (present)		
CENTURY	CALENDAR ROUND	GREGORIAN	CENTURY	
		1711 +		
5th =	460 -100 =	100	= 18th	
		1811 +		
4th (Haab) =	**360 -100 =**	100	**= 19th**	**opens 1st seal**
		1911 +		
3rd (Tzolkin) =	**260 -100 =**	100	**= 20th**	**opens 2nd seal**
		2011 +		
2nd =	**160 -100 =**	100	**= 21st**	**opens 3rd seal**
		2111 +		
1st (Long Count) =	**60 - 49 =**	49	**= 0**	**opens 4th seal (03-20-2012)**

(fig. 64).

In chapter six, we discussed the concept of 2012. We demonstrated how to compensate for the Long Count by adding nine years to the calculation. This led us to determine the long-awaited 2012 to be the year 2021. The Mayan people were obsessed with the year 2021. They understood the reciprocal changes that would occur in the last kin (18 years) for the Age of Pisces (2021 - 2039). The Calendar Round provides codes that corroborate these changes that are hidden within the present calendar for the years 2012, 2021, 2025.

We begin with the numerical date which corresponds with the start of the revolt in Tunisia on 12-17-2010. Each digit for the month and the day is added together to derive at the sacred Mayan number 11 which is added to 2010, and the year 2021 emerges. By 2012, with the assistance from NATO and U.S air strikes, the Arab-Spring should be gaining momentum and Al Qaeda should be fading out. The momentum shall continue on its own for 10 more years to culminate in the liberation of the remaining Middle Eastern nations after the 2.5 degree shift in the wobble of the earth occurs in the year twenty hundred and twenty-one.

The end to the Tunisian revolt also offers us another glimpse into the near future. We examine the date 01-14-2011 to remove the 114 and add it to 2011 and derive at the year 2125. The present Mayan year 2111 is subtracted from 2125 to derive at the balance of 14 years. Thus, by 2025 (2011+14) after the maximum wobble and the speed of the orbit of the earth reaches normal limits, the Arab Spring will be complete, and the earthquakes and tsunamis and the flooding on the earth will virtually disappear. Then, according to the Long Count, seven years of peace will ensue on the earth. By the year 2032, seven years of war will commence as man will inevitably experience a dramatic shift in world diplomacy that will escalate the tensions between certain of the nations in the diplomatic pantheon to an all time high, and the fear of a threat of a nuclear holocaust will stand at the door step of every individual human being. If this scenario ever unfolds, man will lose his battle, his internal struggle between good and evil, between God and Satan, for man's collective intelligence has far surpassed his spiritual progress and he is programmed for failure. Freedom in the spirit or enslavement within the conscious mind -- how will time decide?

And when the fifth seal becomes open (Revelation 6:9-11), "...I saw under the altar the souls of them [in limbo] that were slain for the word of God [for the truth], and for the testimony [against an Agenda of a Snake] which they held: And they cried with a loud voice, saying, how long, O Lord, holy and true, dost thou not judge and avenge our blood on them [the spirits of El and Isis] that dwell [reincarnate] on the earth. And white robes were given unto every one of them, and it was said unto them, that they should rest yet for a little season [for the remaining 29 years before Aquarius] until their fellow servants also and their brethren, that should be killed, as they were should be fulfilled."

We enter into a symbolic understanding of reincarnation and how it applies to a human beings death. Originally, when a person dies, the Michael spirit becomes released from the 13th dimension – the dimension of consciousness – and enters into a state of spiritual consciousness – a state of the subconscious; however, since the fourth generation came to exist, man's Michael spirit enters into the 14th and 15th dimensions, into a state known as limbo. Those two dimensions originally were the places of solitary confinement for El and Isis, respectively, but the spirits of El and Isis no longer reside there. No! Their spirits reside on earth's 13th dimension, for they through the scientific manipulation of alien and human genes became a part of the human race on earth.

Since the Age of Pisces – the age of the human conscious – man became (through his Michael spirit) the one who lives in limbo, and reincarnation became his only release. Two percent of Michael spirits that enter limbo remain there indefinitely, but the other 98% incarnate on earth within seven years from the moment a human being experiences physical death. El and Isis's spirits incarnate immediately upon physical death, and they incarnate into an elite family line, and they have been perpetuating this cycle for the past 2,200 years; thus the book of Revelation reminds man about the imminent liberation of his Michael spirit from the physical confines of the 13th dimension foretold to occur in the Age of Aquarius.

From a time immersed in hope, filled with recluse and repose, we enter into a dramatic moment, a catastrophic nightmare that is caused by an unforeseen circumstance when the sixth seal is open (Revelation 6:12-17), "And, lo, there was a great earthquake and the sun became black as sackcloth of hair [a contaminated atmosphere], and the moon became as blood [fires on the earth]; And the stars of heaven [Michael, Ra, and Viracocha] fell unto the earth…And the heaven departed as a scroll when it is rolled together; and every mountain and island were moved out of their places. And the kings of the earth [political leaders], and the great men, and the rich men, and the chief captains [generals], and the mighty men [soldiers], and every bondman [prisoner], and every freeman, hid themselves in the dens and in the rocks of the mountains… For the great day [the end to earth's day in consciousness]… has come] ; and who shall be able to stand?"

According to Mayan cosmology, sometime in the last third to the Age of Aquarius (about 3500 AD), a cyclical and natural tragedy will bring an end to all biological life on planet earth, and life as man knows will cease to exist. Before this calamity occurs, man will be given the opportunity to transition his Michael spirit from the 13th dimension of consciousness to the fifth dimension of infinite consciousness. Those who continue to go through repetitive reincarnations will choose to remain on earth's 13th dimension to experience the destruction, the complete obliteration of biological life; then, man will trap his Michael spirit in earth's 14th and 15th dimensions for the next 170,000 years.

Nevertheless, he is reminded the Progenitor of the Universe is aware of man's predicament and has sent over messengers to assist him in the future liberation of his Michael spirit. Man's biblical ancestors referred to the messengers as angels. Twenty-first century man calls them *E.T.* Despite the names or the connotations that man ascribes to the beings inside the UFO or to the ones who emerge from the silent light, one thing becomes perfectly clear; Michael, Ra, and Viracocha first came to earth thousands of years ago to fulfill a rescue plan that will take less than a celestial day. Unfortunately for mankind, it will be thousands of years long. Nevertheless, the messengers are here, and in spite of the trials and the tribulations the world will endure the angels came to earth once again to secretly usher the fifth generation into a new and fulfilled age.

For the Day of Harvest to manifest, the Anglo-Saxon races need to become the third breed from the fourth generation. Through a course of natural consequence, they must assimilate themselves with the Indigenous races to create the fifth generation. It is this very condition that will make it necessary for the Day of Harvest to manifest and nowhere else is this fact made clearer than in the New Testament book of Matthew.

Matthew chapter 13: 24-30, "The kingdom of heaven is likened unto a man which sowed good seed [the seed from Michael] in his field: But while men slept, the enemy [an Agenda of a Snake] came and sowed tares [the seed from the Levite people] among the wheat [the seed from Seth] and went his way. But when the blade was sprung up, and brought forth fruit, then appeared the tares also. So the servants of the householder came and said unto him, Sir, didst not thou sow good seed in thy field? From whence than have it tares? He said unto them, an enemy [the Seven Headed Serpent] hath done this. The servants said unto him, Wilt thou then that we go and gather them up? But he said Nay; lest while yea gather up the tares [the El and Isis spirits] yea root up also the wheat [the Michael spirit] with them. Let both [spirits] grow together until the harvest [when the five families in the human race assimilate genetically into one]: and in the time of harvest [two-thirds of the age of Aquarius (3480 AD)] I will say to the reapers, Gather ye together first the tares, and build them in bundles to burn them: but gather the wheat into my barn."

Matthew chapter 13:37-39 explains the confusing parable, "He that soweth the good seed is the Son of man [children of Seth]; the field is the [three-dimensional] world [of consciousness] the good seed [the indigenous races] are the children [the inheritors] of the kingdom; but the tares [the Levite people] are the children [the inheritors] of the wicked one [an Agenda of a Snake]; the enemy that sowed them is the devil [the Seven Headed Serpent]; the harvest is the end of the [three-dimensional] world; and the reapers are the angels [Michael, Ra, and Viracocha]."

In essence, the Harvest will commence at the start to the Age of Aquarius in 2040 AD when the fifth generation shall begin to proliferate on the earth for the next 900 years assimilating themselves genetically into one race, into one color, into one people – the modern human race. At this point, man will become equal to each other through his race but will remain disproportionate through his Michael spirit. He will be left to choose between the spirit of a Snake (materialism) and the spirit of Michael (immaterialism). Although this decision appears simple, it becomes complex. The spiritual forces of materialism are rooted in El and Isis, and they have genetically manifested themselves within every human being to control each life through the action of sex, and through the pride for money, and it takes no time for us to realize the two ideas are the predetermining factors that drive the will and the spirit of the human conscious today. Now, the seventh seal becomes open (Revelation 8:1) and, "There was silence in heaven [earth's moon] about the space of half an hour [208 years]." The Mayan and biblical apocalypse will become fulfilled in 3480 A.D. two thirds into the Age of Aquarius. An event of the magnitude to end biological life on earth's 13th dimension could not go unnoticed by the inhabitants living inside planets within the solar system, in this case it is the Archangel (Elohim) who is living on the moon and is monitoring the situation from the first dimension. Elohim bequeathed the Mayan calendar to man in the hope that someone will be able to explain and apply the Mayan calendar to the events in the 21st century.

If intelligent life exists outside of the earth, why can't science find any evidence to support life on the moon or on the other planets within the solar system? The reason is very simple. Science seeks for evidence in the wrong dimension. Spirits occupy a different dimension than man. Aliens live in the fifth dimension, and angels live in the first. However, man is the only life-form with an angelic spirit to reside within the 13th dimension which is reserved exclusively for the animals.

For every five ages delineated in the Mayan Calendar, a celestial day in consciousness occurs. This means each of the 17 planets experiences a day in consciousness once every 170,000 years (17 x 10,000). This also means earth's 13th dimension teemed with biological life approximately 170,000 years ago. We will come to see in the next chapter how man's concept of time and history is forever altered. Man applies the concept of time through an illusion, but the Mayans applied the concept of time through the cyclical ages. Therefore, at the end of the Age of Aquarius and for the next 10,000 years that begin, Venus will sustain biological life in its 13th dimension.

Now, Revelation chapter 12:1-4 continues, "There appeared a great wonder in heaven; a woman [earth as mother nature] clothed with [heated by] the sun, and the moon under her feet [in her control], and upon her head a crown of twelve stars [earth is ruled by the Nephilim]: And she being with child [the 5th generation] cried, travailing in birth, and pained to be delivered. And there appeared another wonder in heaven; and behold a great red dragon [an Agenda of a Snake], having seven heads [the Seven Headed Serpent] and ten horns [the Tenth Planet] and seven crowns [the seven continents] upon his heads. And his tail drew the third part of the stars of heaven [the Nephilim and the Huzin angels], and did cast them to the earth [to reincarnate on the 13th dimension]: and the dragon [an Agenda on earth] stood before the woman which was ready to be delivered, for to devour her child [the fifth generation] as soon as it was born." There will come a time, by the first-third of the Age of Aquarius (2040 + 720 = 2760 A.D.), when the fifth generation will become the modern human race. The spirits of El and Isis will continue to reincarnate through their elite family line but will lose the control of the fifth generation's human conscious.

But an Agenda will not surrender control of the conscious mind without a fight and eventually (Revelation 12:7-9), "There was war in heaven [on the moon]: Michael and his angels [Ra and Viracocha] fought against the dragon [the Seven Headed Serpent]; and the dragon fought and his angels, and prevailed not; neither was their place found anymore in heaven. And the great dragon [the spirits of El and Isis] was cast out [of the world of consciousness], that old [Seven Headed] serpent, called the Devil, and Satan [who brought the condition of evil] which deceiveth the whole world [through the human conscious]: he was cast out into the earth, and his angels [the spirits of El and Isis] were cast out [into earth's limbo] with him."

No later than 2760 A.D. (2040 + 720) the spirits of El and Isis will separate from the human mind and the Day of Harvest will end. Man's Michael spirit will end its long but steady climb to spiritual freedom. The Day of Harvest represents that great moment in human history when the deadline for the Ra Agenda is met, and man will make contact with his Michael spirit if he chooses to do so. By the first-third of the Age of Aquarius, the human conscious will be released from the bondage El and Isis has inflicted on the Michael spirit, and man no longer will be destined to live with them as human beings in the 13th dimension. Man will have 720 years to reach the stage of spiritual development that makes it possible for him to transition his Michael spirit into the fifth dimension before physical life on earth's 13th dimension becomes extinct. Those of us who choose the path to materialism will reincarnate on earth and will continue to do so until the end to earth's day in consciousness occurs in 3480 AD (2040 + 1440). Those of us who choose the path to a spiritual transformation will transition from the physical to the spiritual state to no longer require the need for a physical body. Man will transition to a fifth dimension during his sleep, for it becomes the Michael spirit's moment when the conscious mind has been shut off.

The condition called sleep occurs not in the 13th dimension but in the fifth dimension within man's mind. This fact becomes obvious once we briefly compare time to the sleep and to the dream state. When someone sleeps without dreaming the conscious mind remains aware of the time that has elapsed; however, when a person dreams the person's conscious mind becomes unaware of the time. The normal human being experiences an average of three dreams in a night whether or not she or he remembers them, and the average dream lasts 20-30 minutes. If this is true, why does man's conscious mind think a dream that lasted approximately 30 minute lasted most of the night, and why would someone who takes a short nap wake-up to discover that it was an hour long when it felt as if only a few minutes had elapsed? This difference between conscious and subconscious between sleep and the dream state becomes the key to understanding the UFO phenomenon man calls missing time.

The state called sleep can't occur in the conscious mind because the conscious mind, with the exception of our dreams, can't remember the sleep period because it becomes turned off. Sleep occurs in the fifth dimension – the dimension of the infinite consciousness. In essence, thought (which produces an electrical response to a physical stimulus) becomes a manifestation from the 13th dimensional energy that transforms itself in the fifth dimensional world of the human mind. Man's human mind exists within the left-brain and is destined to die along with the human body, but man's Michael spirit exists within the right brain and is destined to live forever.

Therefore, after the end of biological life on earth's 13th dimension, the spirits of El and Isis including the remaining Michael spirits will become trapped on earth's 14th and 15th dimensions. Then, John sees (Revelation 21:2), "The holy city, new Jerusalem, coming down from God." At long last, Elohim will have sent Michael to gather the tares.

Then John writes that an angel (Revelation 21:10), "carried me [him] away in the spirit to a great and high mountain, and shewed me [him] that great city, the holy Jerusalem, descending out of heaven [the moon] from God. Revelation chapter 21:11, "...And her light was unto a stone most precious, even like a jasper stone, clear as crystal." An enormous, gigantic, incredible UFO will land on earth near the end to the Age of Aquarius to begin transporting a percentage of the animals to the planet Venus where they will begin to proliferate. The human species will remain behind to suffer the catastrophic consequences with the fallen angels. Thus, for the next 170,000 years, man will be left with no choice but to live in exile with the fallen angels.

CHAPTER NINE

The Epic of Creation

In 1976, after the Viking 1 and then the Viking 2 spacecrafts left earth and traversed through space to reach the Planet Mars, NASA engineers entered them into an orbit around the red planet. As they orbited Mars, from an average distance of some 1,000 miles above the surface, the orbiters obtained a series of high-resolution photographic images. As they relayed the information through space, teams of anxious and eager scientists waited on earth to retrieve and to decode the data.

This was to be the first opportunity for the scientists at NASA to obtain a close-up image of the neighboring planet. As the NASA scientists evaluated the information from the pictures raining into the data bank, they were amazed at the clarity of the images that scanned in. After the excitement and the commotion from the scientists dissipated, they began to reveal the most spectacular images of Mars to the media, but to the particular set of photographs that are simply dubbed as the face, NASA has deemed unworthy for the public approval. They along with the other pictures were quickly filed-away, locked inside a cabinet and forgotten.

Some ten years later the pictures remerged from the cover page of Richard Hoagland's controversial book --*The Monuments of Mars.* He introduced the two investigators (Die Pietro and Molenaar) who were responsible for locating the pictures from NASA's files and for revealing to the media and therefore to the world the face's existence. They drew attention to an image that was photographed in the "Cydonia" region of Mars of an anomaly on the landscape that resembles the face of a humanoid which is shrouded half in shadow.

The face displays the features of an eye, a nose, and a mouth. Those parts of the face are not covered in shadow but are shrouded in light.

(fig. 65)

When the pictures were examined by Mark J. Carlotto, a computer analyst, who put the images of the face through computer enhancement, the face revealed a pupil within the eye which appears to shed a teardrop. Carlotto enhanced the area in the face's mouth and demonstrated teeth. Finally, to estimate its size, the images were subjected to a mathematical computation and the face on Mars was determined to be over one mile long.

Because of the immense size of the face, the anomaly was quickly dismissed as a simple trick of light and shadow that was cast on top of a mountain. In fact, in 1998, NASA released newer images of the face, taken from the Mars Reconnaissance Orbiter (MRO), which shows it to be the result of erosion on a mountain. However, subsequent images of the face show it to continue to be there. Furthermore, the organization called Meta Research has determined:

1. The pictures taken by the MRO were taken from a low perspective angle to the west as opposed to overhead as in the Viking images.
2. In the Viking images the sun shines from low west while in the MRO images the sun shines from low southeast.
3. The Viking images contain a normal variation in the gray scale level, but the MRO images are inadequate for providing contrast between the adjacent features. The result is simple. The MRO images are insufficient for us to derive at a definite conclusion as to the authenticity of the face. The question remains unanswered.

However, author Richard Hoagland introduced the face not as an isolated anomaly standing on Mars to be explained-away as an illusion caused by a trick of light and shadow, but as an intelligently built structure that mathematically aligns with other anomalous structures standing nearby which together forms an ancient settlement.

Armed with a magnifying lens in his hand, Hoagland meticulously scoured the photographic images that NASA dubbed the face to derive at the conclusion that it and the anomalous structures standing nearby were the remains from an ancient settlement still standing on the planet Mars. He measured three anomalies that were aligned mathematically to each other. Hoagland called them the D&M pyramid, the city, and the face.

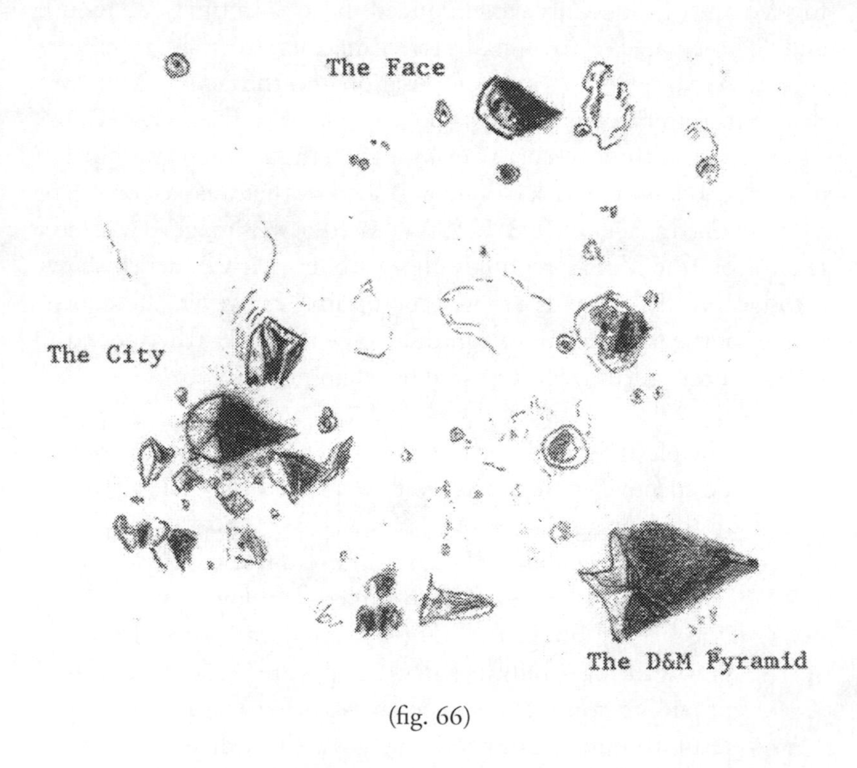

(fig. 66)

Clearly, the face on Mars to some degree seems to resemble the sphinx on earth, and like the sphinx in Egypt, the face on Mars has a pyramid adjacent to it. A Picture from earth of ancient Egyptian architecture comes as no shock for us to witness but to encounter pictures taken on Mars of a similar architecture but in a grandeur scale is simply mind-boggling.

If the face on Mars is created artificially, it implies that there exists a connection between Mars and earth, but a connection between them is impossible because Mars at the present time shows no evidence to sustain biological life in the past -- or does it. Pictures, obtained from the MRO in 2006, indicates Mars to have brown streaks inside craters during the spring and summer. In the colder seasons, the streaks are gone. This to some scientists is an indication of water. In 2008, the probe called Phoenix, landed on the Martian North Pole. Pictures that were obtained show strange blobs on the struts of the landing pads of the Phoenix which according to some experts resembles ice. Yet whether Mars can sustain life in the present doesn't matter. We contend that every planet within the solar system experiences a day in consciousness – many times over! And the planets take turns when they do so – all seventeen of them!

If the earth is the only planet in the solar system to sustain biological life always, it will make the existence of the 16 other planets that exist apart from it useless. Never can there be a balance between the 17 planets and the sun to allow for biological life to exist in any of them, but the balance does exist, and the planets do take turns providing biological life in the 13th dimension.

As we understand the solar system to exist, there are a total of 17 planets that orbit the sun from the three different planes of the ecliptic,

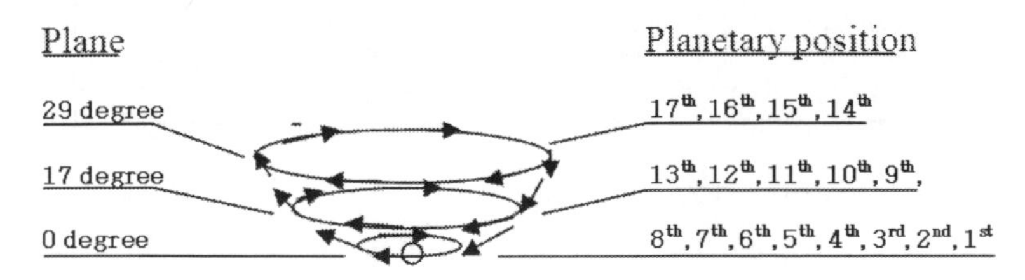

(fig. 67) The arrangement of the solar system, the 17 planets, and the three different planes of the ecliptic.

and the 17 orbits from those planets are so intricately interconnected with each other that every 10,000 years a planet that is in the 12th position (which the ancient Sumerians named Nibiru – the planet of the crossing) crosses into the orbit of the planet closest to the sun (Mercury).

Currently, mankind finds itself in this predicament as the encroaching Planet Nibiru is sending out a gravitational field that will eventually free Mercury from the gravitational hold of the sun's first orbit and will begin to move it toward the second position occupied by the planet Venus while Nibiru takes the first position. In the allotted time, Venus, also because of the approaching gravitational field of Mercury, will leave the second orbit to begin moving toward the third position occupied by the planet earth; thus, the order of the planets will continue to systematically shift positions in their orbits while maintaining the original distances between themselves until the 17th position becomes filled to which a state of homo-stasis is reached.

One thousand, four hundred years later the cycle will repeat when the planet in the 12th position and the planet in the first position become the two planets to orbit closest to the sun. Because of the electromagnetic pull from the sun and the increased velocity the 12th Planet will achieve by entering into a zero ecliptic, it will move toward the first orbit from a position opposite the other planets and from the other side of the sun. Eight thousand and six hundred years later the 17th position becomes complete, and the shift after 1,400 years, will prepare to repeat.

17 planets x 506 years =	8,602 = (end Gemini to end Pisces)
Homeostasis =	1,400 = (2/3 Aquarius)
Total =	10,002

(fig. 68) Ten years are left for homeostasis to end in 2021 for the last 1,400 years that remain in earth's day in consciousness.

This is exactly the position earth is in today.

Now, the energy from a planet originates from the sun and continues as the source of the planets gravitational field. The difference in the speeds among the planets that lie in the three different ecliptic planes is inversely proportional to the angle of the degree; the greater the angle that comes from the ecliptic, the slower is the velocity of the planet and the lesser the angle that comes from the ecliptic, the faster is the velocity of the planet. When a planet comes from the eighth position (in the zero ecliptic) and approaches a planet from the ninth (a 17 degree ecliptic), the speed of its orbit will decrease, and when a planet comes from the 17th position (in the 29 degree ecliptic) and moves toward a planet from the twelve (a 17 degree ecliptic), the speed of its orbit will increase.

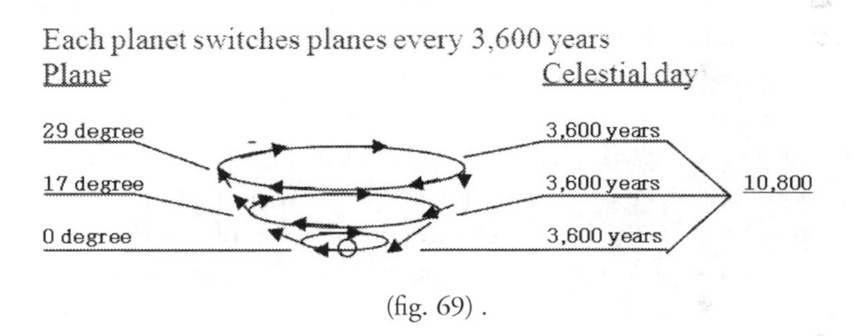

(fig. 69) .

The difference of the speeds among the planets from the three planes of the ecliptic and the gravitational push the sun exerts on the 12th Planet constitutes the forces behind the shift of a planet and leads to the calculation of the precession of the equinoxes.

The epic of creation, *The Enuma Elish,*

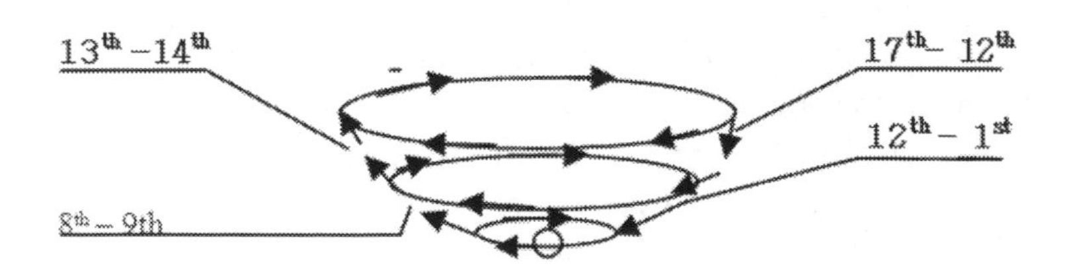

(fig. 70) Positions of planets that shift planes in the ecliptic.

handed down to man since approximately one thousand B.C., contains the creation story of the Asteroid Belt, and it has long been surmised to relate to the creation of the solar system. Yet it does not. The *Enuma Elish* describes a battle in space between the Princes of Light and the princes of darkness. The symbolic battle takes precedent over 9,000 years ago when Lahamu is the next planet destined to inherit a day in consciousness and is about to fix into the third orbit of Mars, and Mars is destined to begin its journey to fix into its present fourth orbit.

This celestial battle between the planets survived the grinding, pulverizing, wheels of time to remain alive in saga as a war between the gods (planets in the zero-ecliptic) and an adversary Tiamat (possessor of the third orbit). She originated from the pantheon of gods and attempted to usurp the newly endowed third orbit of the approaching Lahamu. Since the ancient times to the present, stories abound about a lost continent and its people that were destroyed in a cataclysmic catastrophe. The earliest legends speak of two such glorious and delightful places of splendor – the lost city of Atlantis (whose ruins are located in the Cydonia region of Mars) and the lost continent of Mu (destroyed when Mars' eleven moons collided with Lahamu). Not surprisingly, with the exception of Mummu (Venus) that was saved from imminent destruction when it fixed with Lahamu's second orbit, both Lahamu and Lahmu, (planets that were destroyed) bore the legendary and cataclysmic name of Mu.

So we search for an explanation, for a source of reference for the shifting of the planets orbits, and we find it within the 3,000 year old Babylonian Version of the epic of creation the Enuma Elish (tablet 1:1-13), "When above the heavens [the moon] had not (yet) been named, (And) below the earth had not (yet) been called by a name ; (When) Apsu primeval [the sun], their begetter, Mummu [First Planet], (and) Tiamat [Mars in the third orbit], she who gave birth to them all [eleven moons], (Still) mingled their waters [gravitational forces] together, And no pasture land had been formed (and) not (even) a reed marsh was to be seen; When none of the (other) gods [planets] had been brought into being [positioned], (When) they had not (yet) been called by their name(s, and their) destinies [orbits] had not (yet) been fixed, (At that time) were the gods [positions of the planets] created within them. Lahmu [fourth Planet] and Lahamu [Second Planet] came into being; they were called by (their) names. Even before they had grown up (and) became tall, Anshar [Saturn's] and Kishar [Neptune's orbits] were created; they surpassed them [Jupiter and Uranus]. They lived many days, adding years (to days)."

We enter a time when the second orbit (Lahamu) within the zero-ecliptic is ready to leave its second position to begin its 505 year-long journey to the third. Mars will leave its fourth position at the appropriate time while the other planets that proceed (Jupiter, Saturn, Uranus, Neptune) wait to follow; thus, Tiamat (Mars) will end its day in consciousness, and Lahamu – destined for the third orbit – will begin.

However, Tiamat's eleven moons vehemently oppose her decision to abandon the third position, so "The divine brothers gathered [their gravitational forces] together. They disturbed Tiamat and assaulted(?) [discombobulated] their keeper; Yea, they disturbed the inner parts [mantle], of Tiamat (tablet 1: 21-23)."

Meanwhile, Lahamu left the second position to take a 505 year-long journey to the third. While at the same time, the erratic orbits from Tiamat's moons were putting dramatic stress on her inner core. Meanwhile, the other planets that sat waiting at zero degrees from the ecliptic knew the game and complained to Apsu (the sun) to stop the erratic orbits of Tiamat's eleven moons which were intended to prevent Lahamu from achieving its day in consciousness. But, "Apsu could not diminish their clamor, And Tiamat was silent in regards to their [behavior] (tablet 1:25, 26)."

With no remedy in hand, with Apsu secretly conspiring with Mummu to attain the third orbit, the unsatisfied gods, elected Ea (the Fourth Planet), the one of supreme understanding, to battle Tiamat. "He made and established against it a magical circle [in the zero- ecliptic] for all [the remaining moons to follow with him]." He skillfully composed his overpowering, holy incantation. He recited it and thus caused (it) to be upon the water [the gravitational field of the sun]. He poured out sleep upon him [Apsu], (so) (that) he slept soundly (tablet 1:61-64)." Ea somehow overcame the gravitational field of the sun and re-routed the Fourth Planets direction creating a new but opposite path for the remaining moons to follow with him.

To "Mummu [the first Planet] ... he [Ea] loosened his [Mummu's] band [hold on the third orbit] (and) tore [off] his tiara [his chance]. [Then,] Mummu he shut in [the second position] (and) barred (the door) [of the third orbit] against him (tablet1:67, 70)." Now, with Mummu fixed in the second position, Ea establishes his new abode in the 12th position – the Twelve Planet (tablet 1:76-79), "He named it Apsu and appointed (it) for shrines. (There) Ea (and) Damkina, his wife, dwelt in splendor, "In the chamber of fates [Nibiru--the planet of the crossing], the abode of destinies." With Ea no longer living in the fourth Planet (Lahmu) it broke free from the gravitational hold of the sun's fourth position then began moving retrograde toward the third orbit of Tiamat, at the same time, Mars (Tiamat) began moving ante-grade toward the fourth position.

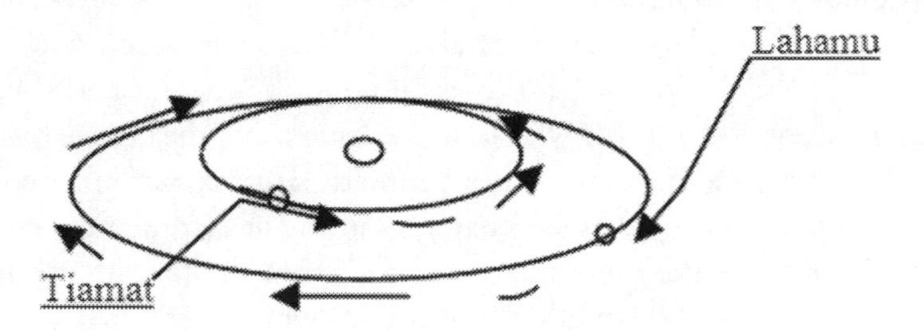

(fig. 71).

But before Tiamat would leave to the fourth position, her eleven moons complained (tablet 1:115-117), "Disturbed is thine interior, and we cannot rest. Remember(?) Apsu thy spouse [the sun], And Mummu [the First Planet], who were vanquished; thou dwellest alone." Convinced by her sons' pleas to retaliate, and with the Fourth Planet on its way toward the third position, Tiamat said to, "the gods in the midst of [her]. [....] let us make war, against the gods let us [....]! They [separated themselves (?)] and went to the side of

Tiamat (tablet1:126-128). Then, with the Gods on her side, Tiamat, "exalted Kingu [Mars' largest moon]; in their midst she made him great. She gave him the tablet of destinies [the third orbit], she fastened (it) upon his breast (tablet 1:147,156)."

Thus, an Agenda on the third planet Mars attempted to steal the third orbit indefinitely by arranging for Kingu's position to take-over the third orbit when Mars began moving toward the fourth. With the addition of Kingu as an 18th planet a state of equilibrium was reached between the planets and the sun, and now the passageways into and out of the three ecliptic planes that are located on the opposite ends of the solar system became closed. Kingu had usurped the tablet of destinies, and by permanently fixing himself to the third orbit, he was now destined for a day in consciousness.

Again, the outer gods convened with Ea in council to choose his valiant son Marduk (the Fourth Planets largest moon) to battle Tiamat and to stop Kingu; however, Marduk had a request for Ea (Tablet 2:123,124,127), "If I am indeed to be your avenger, To vanquish Tiamat and to keep you alive... May I through the utterance of my mouth determine the destinies [the third orbit], instead of you."

While still maintaining their own orbits around Lahmu, its two moons began to travel with Lahmu in a retrograde path to the 3rd position and on a head-on collision with Tiamat, who was now halfway to the fourth position. But to vanquish Tiamat, Marduk, who was now orbiting with five other moons around the Fourth Planet, asked to inherit the third orbit. Ea agreed. And, "He [Marduk] made a net [by combining the moons gravities] to inclose Tiamat within (it), (And) had the four winds [the combined gravitational energy of a moon from Jupiter, from Saturn, from Uranus, and from Neptune] take hold that nothing of her might escape; The south wind, the north, wind, the east wind, (and) the west wind (tablet 4:41-43)." As the Fourth Planet neared Mars orbit, "The Lord took a direct (route) and pursued his way; Toward the place of raging Tiamat he set his face. Then the gods r[un] about him, the gods run about him (tablet 4:59,60,63). With Tiamat's moons seemingly missing a head-on collision with the moon called

Marduk, with Tiamat surrounded in the four directions by the four winds, with no recourse but to proceed forward – Marduk and Tiamat, "pressed on to single combat, they approached for battle. The Lord spread out his net [the six moon's gravitational fields] and enmeshed her; The Evil wind [the sixth moon], following after, he let loose in her face. When Tiamat opened her mouth to devour him, He drove in the evil wind, in order that (she should) not (be able) to close her lips. The raging winds filled her belly; Her belly became distended, and she opened wide her mouth. He shot off an arrow, and it tore her interior; It cut through her inward parts, it split (her) heart [core] (tablet 4:94-102)."

Vanquished by Marduk, "Her [gravitational] band broke up, her host [Mar's eleven moons] dispersed. As for the gods her helpers, who marched at her side, They trembled for fear (and) faced about. They tried to break away to save their lives, (But) they were completely surrounded [by the four winds], (so that) it was impossible to flee. He imprisoned them and broke their weapons. In the net [the new gravitational field] they lay and in the snare [the retrograde orbit] they were; They hid in the corners (and) were filled with lamentation; They bore his wrath; being confined in prison (tablet 4:106-114). " To Tiamat's eleven moons (tablet 4:116-118), "The host of demons that marched impetuously before her, He cast (them) into fetters (and) [tied(?)] their arms [to-gether(?)]; With (all) their resistance, [he tr]ampled (them) underfoot." The moons that had become attracted to Tiamat's orbit were now fragmented and dispersed in a direction opposite of the planets to become the comets – the only members in the solar system to orbit the sun in a direction opposite; thus, the comets present paths represent Lahmu's retrograde orbit.

Then, (tablet 4:119-121), "As for Kingu, who had become chief among them, He bound [stopped] him [from rotating on his axis] and counted him among the dead gods [captured moons]. He took from him the tablet of destinies [the third orbit], which was not his rightful position.

After Lahmu revolved around the sun in an orbit halfway between the present position of Mars and earth, Marduk comes back (tablet 4:128-132), "to Tiamat, whom he had subdued. The

Lord trod upon the hinder part of Tiamat, And with his unsparing club he split (her) skull [fractured Mars internal diameter]. He cut the arteries of her blood [ended Mars' day in consciousness]. And caused the north wind to carry (it) to out-of-the-way places [to its present fourth orbit]." As Mars neared the halfway point to the position it occupies today, Marduk (Tablet 4:137-138), "split her open like a mussel (?) [Lahmu, the Fourth Planet, smashed head-on into Tiamat breaking her] into (two parts); Half of her he set in place and formed the sky (therewith) as a roof [the Asteroid Belt]."

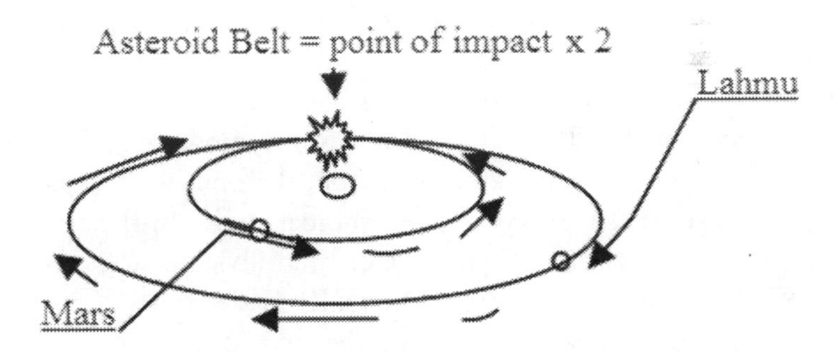

(fig. 72) Creation of the Asteroid Belt.

By destroying Lahmu and bringing the number of planets down to 17, the entrances to and exits out of the three planes at the opposite ends of the ecliptic were re-open and Marduk (Tablet 5:6-9), "founded the station [the passage] of Nibiru [through the 12th position] to make known their [the planets'] duties(?) [positions]. That none might go wrong [wander] (and) be remiss [left out of a day in consciousness], He established the stations [passage] of Enlil [through the 13th position] and Ea [through the 17th position] together with it. He opened gates [re-opened the three planes to the eclipses] on both sides."

This epic story of creation carries far-reaching implications for the destiny of man since it describes how the angels ended a day in consciousness for Kingu, and it explains how the asteroid belt was formed. Today, as we contemplate the Asteroid Belt, we are unaware it is a remnant of the celestial collision that occurred between the planet Lahmu and Mars. Thereafter, Lahmu and half of Mars formed the Asteroid Belt, while the other half of Mars fixed with the fourth position taking with it the remaining two moons of Lahmu to its new orbit.

Lahamu (the Second Planet), was well on its way to the third orbit when its gravitational field began to push Kingu to the moon's present orbit. Then Lahamu traveling in an ante-grade direction entered into several head-on collisions with the remaining moons of Mars which had dispersed in the retrograde direction to escape, and they became shattered into pieces. At the end, Lahmu's moon (Marduk) replaced the vacant third orbit and inherited a day in consciousness. Thus, earth's moon – Kingu -- is a satellite that originated from Mars, and earth is a moon – Marduk – that originated from Lahmu. The ten remaining moons of Mars, the gods that accompanied Tiamat to battle, the ones who turned in desperation in the final moments of combat to flee in the opposite direction, collided with the planet Lahamu to become the comets.

We distance ourselves from the tablet of destinies to re-focus on the face on Mars and combine the two ideas to the Mayan Calendar which correlates earthly time to celestial. Until man views the Mayan Calendar, the tablet of destinies, and the UFO mystery through the guise of celestial time, he will remain lost in the product of earthly time, for the difference between the first dimension and the 13th are theoretically immeasurable. Although time is irrelevant to the angels, they use celestial time to track the events that are occurring on the 13th dimension of the planet on the third orbit.

The Mayan Calendar depicts a celestial day to be exactly five ages. Each age is determined by the precession to be exactly 2,160 years long. In the Mayan Calendar a day in consciousness is equal to 10,000 years, but in the Precession of the Equinoxes, a celestial day is equal to five ages or 10,800 years long. This means that earth's day in consciousness (10,000/2,160) is exactly four point six Mayan ages long.

In order to compare earthly time to the product of celestial time, the five ages in the Mayan calendar are multiplied by the number five (5 x 2,160), to derive at the sum of 10,800 – eight hundred years in excess of a celestial day. Then, we subtract the four ages which mankind has already experienced -- Gemini, Taurus, Aires, Pisces -- from a day in consciousness (10,000 - 8,600), and we derive at 1,400 as the approximate number of years that remain within earth's day in consciousness. If 1,400 is subtracted from 2,160, we will derive at 760 years which reveals the last third of the Age of Aquarius; this represents a time when mankind will no longer experience biological life in earth's 13th dimension (10,800 - 10,000). Those remaining 760 years in the Age of Aquarius will belong to Venus when it will fix itself into earth's present orbit.

If we follow the signs of the zodiac back in time, to some 9,000 years ago, it will be the same in the last third of the Age of Gemini when earth will fix into the third orbit to begin a day in consciousness, and Mars begins its long journey to the fourth orbit. We have determined the biblical flood is not a punishment that is handed down on man by an angry, oppressive, and vindictive God. Rather, we have shown the flood to be a cyclical and natural calamity that occurs every 10,000 years to the planet that occupies the third orbit. In 1,400 years Venus will occupy the third orbit, and earth will begin its journey toward the fourth position of Mars.

Therefore, the *Enuma Elis*h establishes a time some 9,000 years ago when Mars is still fixed to a third position from the sun to become the last planet to sustain biological life in the third orbit. The remnants in the Cydonia region of Mars that were photographed by the Viking spacecrafts in 1976 and identified by author Richard Hoagland in "The Monuments of Mars" were created about 18,200 years ago when Mars first occupied the third orbit from the sun, and the face that portrays itself on the Martian landscape belongs to an ancient Egyptian, and the proposed city that Hoagland spotted nearby the vicinity of the Face belongs to the lost city of Atlantis. Although the ancient Egyptian people were created in Jupiter approximately 26,000 years ago at the end of the Age of Pisces, an Agenda took them to Mars at the end of Jupiter's day in consciousness some 18,600 years ago.

Thus, the Babylonian epic of creation explains how a day in consciousness on the third orbit of Mars was about to end for an

Agenda, and like the well designed modern-day science fiction thriller the plot thickens when an Agenda steals the third position by placing Kingu permanently within the third orbit. For as a consequence of living within a 13th dimension and since the past 200,000 years, the Nephilim, the Huzin angels, the Seven Headed Serpent, and the Nation of Israel, followed the tablet of destinies from planet to planet. Now, an Agenda devised a scheme, a plan to usurp the tablet of destinies and remain living within Kingu indefinitely. Again, as a consequence to the fallen angels, over 9,000 years ago, chaos ensued within the solar system as the orderly shift of planets was disrupted, but once again, the fallen angels suffered consequences for their deeds when Elohim imprisoned El and Isis on earth for an eternity for unsuccessfully attempting to usurp the 3rd orbit. Now, trapped on earth's 14th and 15th dimensions forever, El and Isis lost the battle, but in the process they also trapped man's Michael spirit. When their spirits possessed the brains of the Girgashite people, they became one with the human bodies, and they immediately lost their identity through the conscious mind, and their 14th and 15th dimensional spirits became trapped in the 13th dimensional world on earth. As time is ending for them in the 13th dimension, it is also ending for us.

The book of Genesis states that Noah was born 500 years before the flood which as we ascertain occurred in the last third of the Age of Gemini. This means that if man travels back in time through the Precession of the Equinoxes, to some 19,000 years ago, he will pass through the nine ages starting from the end of the present Age of Pisces back to the end of the Age of Scorpio. Mars will have just occupied the third orbit. Thus, the Ancient Egyptian (Enki) and the Kenizzite people (Enlil) migrated to earth 100 years before Mar's day in consciousness would end to become known on earth as the Egyptian (line of Seth) and Sumerian people (line of Cain). An Agenda transported them to earth over 9,000 years ago just before Mars ended its day in consciousness 600 years after Noah was born.

The Bible remains silent as to the 100 years of Noah's life which lead up to the flood. We contend the missing 100 years in Noah's life, the years between his 500th and 600th birthday, represents the only time in the solar system when the approaching Second and the departing Third Planet simultaneously could maintain conditions that are suitable for the development of biological life in their 13th dimensions; the Third Planet is just beginning plant life, and the Fourth is just ending it. On Mars 13th dimension, during the missing 100 years of Noah's life, the Nation of Israel, the Kenizzite, the ancient Egyptian people along with seven pairs of each species of animal were transported to earth by El and Isis where the Seven Headed Serpent awaited. After the biblical deluge ended on Mars, earth's day in consciousness began, and 350 years later (Noah's age after the flood) the second generation began to proliferate on the earth.

Noah	**Age**	**Planet**
Age before flood	500	Mars
Missing years	100	Transition period
Age after flood	350	Earth

(fig. 73).

On earth, before the flood, during the missing 100 years to Noah's life, El and Isis procreated the Kenite people through the genetic manipulation of genes from a mixture of the newly arrived Egyptian and Sumerian people, so it becomes only proper that through the eyes of the first true earthlings – the Kenite people – man gets his first glimpse of earth through a pre-deluged world.

According to the "*Mayan Book of the Dawn of Life the Pupol Vuh*" by author Dennis Tedlock, at the end of part one, life begins for the Kenite (Mayan) people, "This Was When There Was Just A Trace Of Early Dawn on the face of the earth, there was no sun [covered by the dark clouds filled with water vapor]. But there was one who magnified himself; Seven Macaw [the Seven Headed Serpent] is his name. The sky-earth [moon and earth] was already there, but the face of the sun-moon was clouded over [from 24 hours of darkness]. Even so, it is said that his light provided a sign for the people who were flooded."

On earth, the Seven Headed Serpent [Seven Macaw] continued the mating ritual for an Agenda of a Snake, but two brothers, the gods Hunahpu and Xbalanque, saw the imminent evil in the creation of the human race. In South America, towering high on top the Peruvian Andies, immediately after the flood, immediately after earth fixed into the third orbit, the second family, the Egyptian and the Kenite and the Kenizzite people, were being mated by the Seven Headed Serpent. So the two gods talked (Popol Vuh, Part two, page 89), "It's no good without life, without [the Kenite] people here on the face of the earth." They understood Seven Macaw had sequestered the Kenite people for an Agenda's purpose. The Kenites weren't free to roam on earth. They were placed in the Peruvian Andes specifically to mate. Hunahpu and Xbalanque agreed to remove Seven Macaw from his self-elevated position that decreed him above every living thing on earth. He was depicted as a Macaw perched above on a tree branch.

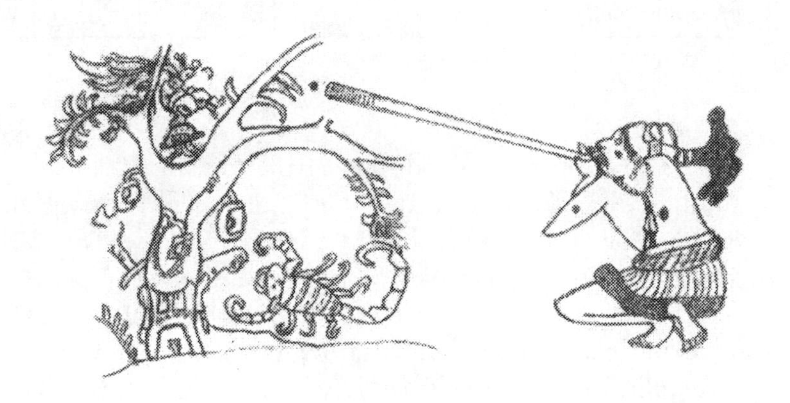

(fig. 74) Classic Maya painting

Seven McCaw is shown perched atop a fruit tree. Hiding to the right is the god Hunahpu in the act of shooting Seven McCaw. The Scorpion represents the end of the Age of Scorpio. The toppling of Seven McCaw signifies when an Agenda lost permanent control of the third orbit to be confined on earth's 8th, 14th, 15th dimensions for eternity.

One day Hunahpu shot him in the jaw with a blowgun. Macaw suffered a broken jaw and collapsed down to the ground. Never again would he regain his elevated status.

This symbolic story commemorates the moment the Seven Headed Serpent lost control of the third orbit's 13th dimension to become exiled on earth forever. However, Seven Macaw was exiled only after creating the Girgashite people near an end to the Age of Aires and only after creating the conscious mind, so the genes from the line of Cain disseminated with the genes from the line of Seth to the level to allow El and Isis's spirit to manifest in a human body through the genes of the Kenizzite. After the flood, the second family through the mating ritual spread to create the second generation, and the third family spread to create the third.

Now, the total ages of the patriarchs from Adam to Noah when added together sum-up to 8, 575 years. This number corresponds almost exactly to the total number in years (4 x 2,160=8,640) of the four previous ages to include the present age – end Gemini, end Taurus, end Aires, and end Pisces; however, more significantly 8,575 corresponds almost exactly to the total number in years it will take the 17 planets to shift each of them into their orbits at 505.88 years each (17 x approximate 505 =8,585). When 8,575 is subtracted from (17x505.88=8,599.96), 24.96 years remain that represents a time in this present moment when Nibiru will fix into Mercury's first position in the year 2036,

Number of whole years in a shift	505
Number of whole years x 17 planets	505 x 17 = 8,585
Total amount of patriarch's ages	8,575
Exact number of years in a shift -	505.88 x 17 = 8,599.96
Total amount of patriarch's ages	-8,575
Number of yrs left for Nibiru to shift with Mercury's 1st position	24.96

(fig.75)

and four years later, in the year 2040, the Age of Aquarius will begin.

Since it takes 505.88 years for each planet to complete a shift (8,600 divided by 17), and it takes 1,400 years (in homeostasis) before the cycle repeats, Nibiru will replace Mercury's position in the year 2036 (2011+25) and will begin to orbit the sun in the first position by the year twenty forty. Approximately, 506 years later Mercury will fix with the second position of Venus. Thus, in about 1,037 years [(2x506)+25], Venus will fix with the third position to become the morning star and bring a new Dawn to a Day in consciousness, and earth will begin its 506 year-long journey to the fourth position. Although earth will leave the third position, it will still be able to sustain biological life for 120 more years. This amount is determined by subtracting Noah's age before the flood from the 720 years that remain in the last third of the Age of Gemini (720-600=120), a figure that signifies when the Second Planet fixes to the third orbit. Thus, in 1,345 years (1,440+25-120) earth's day in consciousness will end and biological life in the 13th dimension will be impossible.

Pisces (past)			Aquarius C.E. (future)		
CENTURY	CALENDAR ROUND		GREGORIAN	CENTURY	Event
0 =		2160 - 100 =	40 + 100	= 1st	Nibiru fixes to 1st position
21st =	2060 - 100 =		140 + 100	= 2nd	C.E. 2140
20th = 100	1960 -	1960 - 100 =	240 + 100	= 3rd	
19th =	1860	1860 - 100 =	340 + 100	= 4th	
18th =		1760 - 100 =	440 + 100	= 5th	
17th =		1660 - 100 =	540 + 100	= 6th	Mercury fixes to 2nd (open 5th seal)
16th =		1560 - 100 =	640 + 100	= 7th	C.E. 2640
15th =		1460 - 100 =	740 + 100	= 8th	
14th =		1360 - 100 =	840 + 100	= 9th	
13th =		1260 - 100 =	940 + 100	= 10th	
12th =		1160 - 100 =	1040 + 100	= 11th	C.E. 3140 Venus fixes to 3rd (open 6th seal)
11th =		1060 - 100 =	1140 + 100	= 12th	3260 C.E. end earth's day in consciousness
10th =		960 - 100 =	1240 + 100	= 13th	C.E.3260
9th =		860 - 100 =	1340 + 100	= 14th	
8th =		760 - 100 =	1440 + 100	= 15th	Limited biological life non-sustainable
7th =		660 - 100 =	1540 + 100	= 16th	C.E. 3640 earth fixes to 4th (open 7th seal)
6th =		560 - 100 =	1640 +100	= 17th	
5th =		460 - 100 =	1740 + 100	= 18th	
4th =	360 - 100 =		1840 + 100	= 19th	
3rd =	260 - 100 =		1940 + 100	= 20th	
2nd =	160 - 100 =		2040 + 100	= 21st	
1st =	60 - 11 - 9 =		2140 + 20	= 0	End Aquarius

(fig. 76)

Conclusion

When the Age of Pisces began in 49 B.C., the Levite people already had enforced their religion and their Agenda on the third generation, and man's Michael spirit began to distance itself from the subconscious and fade away to become one with the spirit of consciousness. Now, in the 11th year in the 20th century of the Gregorian calendar, man prepares to enter into the 21st century of the Age of Pisces which is set to occur on the sunrise of September 23 on the day of the autumnal equinox.

This date will correspond exactly to the start of the Mayan year 2131which represents the time when man's lost Michael spirit will begin to separate from his consciousness and begin the slow transformational journey to the subconscious. This new transformation in human consciousness is unfolding before the world's eyes. The world has caught a glimpse of this phenomenon through the events known as the Arab-Spring. This new wave of consciousness will allow the fifth generation to slowly break free from the bonds that disconnected the fourth Generation from the spirit of Michael. Man, from the fourth generation is programmed genetically to live against the will of the spirit of Michael and is conditioned to follow and obey the will of the spirit of consciousness -- so conveniently imposed against his human spirit.

For 2,131 years the fourth generation has sought to explain man's existence in the science of philosophy and unfortunately through the government in religion. These governments dictated how men will live according to ancient customs that were derived at by the human mediators to a territorial god. Though man tries to find his true destiny, he continuously fails because he has no idea that he needs first to liberate the Michael spirit from the confines of his conscious mind, so he is destined to meet-up with the tares at the end to earth's day in consciousness in 1,429 years.

True - man is cut-short from receiving his status as alien life to reside on earth's fifth dimension. Yet how is he to understand that he possesses both the Michael spirit and the El or Isis spirit which resides within his own mind or that his body has become Satan's temple because the human body is a creation from the fallen angel. So the Michael spirit in man remained alone, abandoned, entrapped within his mind, lost within the illusion he calls time and slowly but surely forgotten.

An Agenda knew that Malek is Ra's creation, and that, masculine and feminine Malek were created through the guidelines which are brought forth in the Seven Heavens and are mandated by Elohim and transposed through the will of the Progenitor of the Universe. The angel is allowed through the Seven Heavens to use genes from a species of animal and to implant into them spirit from the angel to create the special life-form which is required for procreation. But the newly created feminine Malek never donated a womb for the procreation of alien life for earth's fifth dimension. No! How could she! Instead, an Agenda of a Snake usurped feminine Malek's capacity for consciousness when it mixed genes from the Amorite with spirit from El to create the ancient Egyptian people almost exactly 25,920 years ago.

With the creation of the Kenizzite people (the line of Cain) and later the ancient Egyptian people (the line of Seth), the perpetual day in consciousness was put into motion, but not until some 9,000 years ago could it begin to imprint time here on earth at the end of the first Age of Gemini when the Mayan (Kenite) people were created. The Kenizzite and the ancient Egyptian people as we know came from the 11th Planet and the planet Jupiter respectively.

The second Age of Taurus passed. Then, at the onset to the third Age of Aires, Viracocha endowed the Mayan people with the Mayan calendar -- astronomical and prophetical knowledge that tells of the origin and of the future and of the destiny of man. This knowledge stayed behind as the Mayans left earth's 13th dimension to become the first human spirits to reside within the fifth. Although the Mayan calendar was carried-over to the fourth generation by the Native American people (to include North, Central, South America and the Caribbean) by the last third to the Age of Pisces (the end of the 15th century A.D.), it was to be forgotten. The Michael spirit of the Native Americans in the fourth generation was the last to degrade in the human race beginning only when the Anglo-Saxon invaded the New World. Some 500 years later, at the start of the 21st century of the Age of Pisces, the spirit of consciousness of the fourth generation is dying, and a new spirit, a fair and universal spirit, will begin to emerge from the fifth generation.

In the fourth generation the Native Americans and the future generations from around the world suffered a horrific blow when an Agenda burned and desecrated almost in entirety the Mayan history and culture when it invaded the New World enslaving the Native Americans within their own lands. Indeed! All that remains, from such a forbidden and tumultuous time in the course of human history, are the three Mayan codices and the highly revered and sacred calendar that is adapted by the following Native American cultures and which man calls the Mayan Calendar.

Still! To no avail and completely unbeknown to him the Mayan Calendar stands as moot testament to the fact that man is a mix from an alien and an animal species, and the book of Genesis delineates how the line of Cain and the line of Seth reflects this mixture.

Then, in 1955, the Ra Agenda re-emerged as the Cherubims Ra, Michael, and Viracocha came to earth to re-evaluate the two genetic lines in the human race. They discovered that humans who descend from the line of Cain contain a higher percentage of genes that originate from the 10th, the 11th, and the 12th Planet than humans who descend from the line of Seth who contain a higher percentage of genes that originate from the planet Pluto. Within this genetic cesspool which is called the human race, genes from the 10th Planet brought forth the Chinese race; genes from the 11th Planet brought forth the white female gender; genes from the 12th Planet brought forth the white male gender, and genes from the Planet Pluto brought forth the Malek race. In addition, the genes from Malek brought forth the black and the brown complexions, and the genes of the Rephaim and the Girgashite people brought forth the white.

Now, since the past 2,131 years, man's El and Isis spirits exist within the frontal lobe of his left brain creating his conscious mind, and his Michael spirit exists within the brain stem creating his human conscious. Because he is not differentiating between them, man has lost contact with his Michael spirit and has become a living breathing soul who is destined to wait until the day of Harvest (A.D. 2040 – 2540) to begin to free his Michael spirit from the confines of his conscious mind.

Man has 529 years to transcend himself from a human soul who lives in a conscious (three-dimensional) world to a spirit who will reside in a fifth dimension. Through man's repeated reincarnations on earth, he will allow his Michael spirit to break free from the confines of his conscious mind and to relocate to the position where it once occupied in the frontal lobe of the right hemisphere of the human brain. Then, man's Michael spirit upon experiencing physical death will transcend from the 14th and 15th dimensions to the fifth.

Two hundred thousand years ago one-third of the seraphim angels fell from their heavenly estates when they choose to create alien life in the wombs of the Huzinite. They did so when Saturn became fixed to the third orbit. One hundred and eighty thousand years ago Lahmu occupied the third orbit, and it was then that Elohim built the Garden of Eden on Lahmu's largest moon (earth), and it was there that Ra created Malek and where the Sons of God mated with Isis.

Thus, the Nephilim and the Huzinite confined the Seven Headed Serpent and themselves to the world of consciousness, so they destined themselves to follow the third orbit while trapped within its 13th dimension. Approximately 190,000 years ago, the three groups shifted from one planet to the next, from the third orbit to the following, from the previous tablet of destinies to the subsequent – destined to live within the 13th dimension. Ra too shifted the seed of Malek along with the seed of the animals from the third orbit to the following, in the attempt to allow Michael and Elohim the opportunity to create alien life on earth's fifth dimension when its day in consciousness would arrive 170,000 years later.

Twenty-five thousand and two hundred years ago Jupiter still occupied the third orbit, and a war was ensuing in the 13th dimension between an Agenda of a Snake and Ra for the possession of Malek. Through this misfortune, the Seven Headed Serpent was able to recover 20 percent of the Malek species. Eight thousand and six hundred years ago Mars left the third orbit en-route to the fourth. An Agenda attempted to usurp the third orbit from Lahamu (the approaching Second Planet) but failed. This brash attempt by an Agenda to permanently control the third orbit not only brought chaos to the otherwise orderly solar system, but also marked the beginning to an end for an Agenda of a Snake. After it was over, El and Isis were exiled to exist within earth's 14th and 15th dimensions, and the Seven Headed Serpent, who created the human race, was exiled to live in the eighth dimension under the earth.

Thus, the urgency to create the human race resulted when an Agenda lost the control of the third orbit, and El's and Isis's spirits were trapped in earth's 14th and 15th dimensions. When the Seven Headed Serpent created the Girgashite people, the group replaced the Michael spirit in Malek's genes with the El and Isis spirits in Limbo; thus, the El and Isis spirits entered into Malek's genes in the 13th dimension and the spirit of Michael remained trapped in Limbo. Now, the spirit of Michael had to incarnate into a human body in the 13th dimension in order to escape Limbo. This act ultimately brought forth the condition of good and evil and caused ancient man to endow the Seven Headed Serpent with the epithet of the Devil, the deriver of evil.

Ever since man's body became the physical embodiment of his El or Isis spirit and ever since his conscious mind became the expression of his entrapped Michael spirit, he started to believe that body and mind are the same. But in reality, man's body belongs to his consciousness (no different than the consciousness of the dog or the cat), and his conscious belongs to his fifth dimensional spirit which is entrapped within man's 13th dimensional mind.

Originally, man's spirit was trapped in the right brain as was the case in the second generation. But as the time passed on, he became a soul (physical spirit) when his Michael spirit became trapped in the brain stem as is the case in the fourth generation. The ancient Egyptian and the Kenizzite people had a brain stem but no left hemisphere; however, with the creation of the Kenite people some 9,000 years ago, the left hemisphere fully emerged.

The Kenite people from the second family of the human race lived by the will of the Michael spirit. They experienced physical reality through a higher sense than the five senses. They sensed physical reality through the unique and special ability called Extra-Sensory Perception (ESP) which was once rooted in the right hemisphere of the human brain.

The second family (ancient Egyptian, Kenite, Kenizzite) required minimal food, water, or sleep in order to physically exist. When the ancient Egyptian, the Kenite, or the Kenizzite experienced biological death, their human spirit didn't go to the 14th or to the 15th dimension as man's spirit does today; theirs went directly to the fifth.

Since the past 2,400 years, the Michael spirit became deceived and became entrapped within the brain stem, and man began to live the physical lifestyle he enjoys today. Man's lifestyle is motivated by the need for sexual pleasure and by the need to acquire wealth and money. He became so emotionally drained, so spiritually disconnected, that he descended into a spiral of spiritual degeneration.

Might there be a lesson for man to learn, so he may begin to progress his human spirit un-impeded toward earth's fifth dimension: the lesson comes from the spiritual ancestors of the second generation. They accepted the consequences of biological death without sadness or gloom and held a glorious celebration that was filled with a profound happiness for the freed Michael (Egyptian, Kenite) or Huzin (Kenizzite) spirit of the deceased person. They knew their Michael or Huzin spirit became free upon biological death to begin an eternal existence in the fifth dimension. However, once the left hemisphere became fully operational, and man inherited the conscious mind, he began to experience the physical loss of a love one with sadness and with gloom and he began to mourn and to grieve the passing.

Six thousand and five hundred years ago man fell headfirst into the trap that was set by an Agenda to confine the liberty of his

Michael spirit. In spite of his religious fervor, his zeal, or his heart-felt acclamations about God and about his destiny, man hasn't yet understood that he is an entrapped spirit.

Ever since the Age of Aires, Michael, Ra, and Viracocha are working diligently to inform man about his helpless plight. But if a day in consciousness in the third orbit equals 10,000 years, it means that only five hours have elapsed since Michael abducted Ezekiel by the river Chebar, and merely seconds have ticked by since Ra staged the incident at Roswell; thus, in the celestial time-span of one day in consciousness, the Ra Agenda will liberate us human souls, yet we will wait for 10,000 years. To put matters into perspective, just imagine, the 1,400 years that remain for man to exist within earth's day in consciousness, represents only three hours for the Ra Agenda. Such is the tremendous difference between earthly and celestial time.

Consequently, the approximate 1,400 years that remains in earth's day in consciousness consists of the time that is left for Nibiru to fix with the first position (29 years as of 2011) plus the time for the shifts of the First and Second Planets to occur (29+2x505) for a total of 1,039 years; then, planet earth will complete the 365 years that remain in its day in consciousness while en-route to the fourth position (1039+365). Earth's 13th dimension will become barren and void of life by the year 3415 (1404+2011). One hundred and forty years later (505-365+3415) in the year 3555 earth will fix to Mar's present fourth position.

As Nibiru comes closer to Mercury's orbit, it will do so from a higher plane in the ecliptic, so its gravitational field will create a disturbance that affects Mercury, Venus, and earth. Nibiru's approaching gravitational field will cause changes on the speed of the earth which will further enhance the degree in its wobble. According to the Long Count Calendar, as seen through the eyes of Precession, in the year 2011, Nibiru will get the closest it can get to the earth from the higher 17 degree ecliptic; then, it will enter into the passageway that leads to the zero-ecliptic and begin a downward journey to the first position. When Nibiru fixes into the first position, in 2021, its approaching gravitational field will create a slowing in the speed of the orbit of the earth as it revolves on its axis which will increase its wobble by two and one-half of a degree (1x2.5).

Those cyclical and predictable events began to manifest themselves within the crust of the earth resulting in shifts of its tectonic plates. The shifts are manifesting themselves on the surface of the earth as earthquakes and on the surface of the ocean as tsunamis, and since 2003, they are increasing in both frequency and in magnitude and will continue to increase until after Nibiru fixes with the first position.

Mankind will enter into the Age of Aquarius by the year 2040 when Nibiru is fixed to Mercury's first position. Mercury will begin the 505 year-long journey toward Venus. After Mercury reaches the second position, Venus will begin its long journey toward earth to inherit its day in consciousness, and the information in the Dresden Codice will be fulfilled. In approximately 1,400 years, the earth will occupy Mars present position and will display the same atmospheric and geologic conditions Mars 13th dimension displays today.

One thousand and thirty-nine years from this present 21st century, Venus will occupy earth's third position, and earth will have 365 years remaining of biological life in its 13th dimension. The El and Isis spirits incarnated on earth who through genetic family lines maintain the power, proliferate the wealth, exploit the expenditure and the luxury of money, will escape from the dying earth in the hope of reaching Venus. Those of us, who remain unaware of our Michael spirits, will be faced with dire consequences, for we will remain trapped within earth's 14th and 15th dimensions for eternity.

Yet the spirits of the fallen angels that live as human beings will escape from the end of earth's day in consciousness. Like the well designed Hollywood script, the seed of the fallen angels will rocket away from the earth into space in the hope of reaching Venus for another day in consciousness. But Michael, Ra, and Viracocha will prevent them and defeat them. Relinquished, in space, the spirits of the fallen angels will plummet down to earth into the 14th and 15th dimensions, and man's Michael spirit will be trapped with the spirits of El and Isis for eternity.

How can man rest assure his Michael spirit will transform itself from the 14th and 15th dimensions into the fifth at the end to the day of Harvest? Man's quest will begin by accepting the human diversity. Man's racial diversity has come about from an Agenda as it put to breed the families from the line of Cain with the families from the line of Seth. In the age of Pisces, the El family (the fourth generation) through the natural course of time would breed with the Ra family (the third generation) for 1,440 years (2/3 of the Age of Pisces) to bring forth the Anglo-Saxon (the third El family from the Levite) and the Indigenous races (the third Ra family from Seth).

The Anglo-Saxon and the Indigenous races have been breeding for over 500 years. In the year 2040, when the Age of Aquarius will officially begin, man will reach the starting point for the breeding of the fifth generation as they grow into adulthood. This will mark the beginning to the day of Harvest as the Michael spirit shall slowly slip away from the bonds of the conditioning process that is placed on it some 2,500 years ago.

Man's Michael spirit now will begin to migrate toward the right hemisphere of the human brain. In five hundred and thirty-four years (505+29), Venus will start its trip toward earth; the day of Harvest will end; the human race will become one race – the modern human race, and man's Michael spirit will be seated in the frontal lobe of the right hemisphere of the human brain. By that time man's spirit will separate from the conscious mind to go through a 180 degree shift and reach the crossroad of the second generation some 6,000 years later.

In the meantime, for man back here in the 21st century, his lessons to escape from earth's dying 13th dimension will only begin, for by the year 2040, his human spirit no longer will require the need to incarnate if it chooses to do so. In order for man's Michael spirit to become disengaged from the cycle of reincarnation, it first needs to dissolve the physical bond that is placed on it by an Agenda.

The time has come for man to discover his true nature. In essence, his body had become Michael's temple when an Agenda initially trapped his Michael spirit within the right hemisphere of the human brain. The body is a physical structure that houses the

Michael spirit, but an Agenda developed man's left-brain to place the spirits of El and Isis within it and to create the conscious mind.

The human body then became the temple for El and Isis, and the right brain, which stands as the temple for Michael, became the mysterious subconscious. Boldly stated, the human body now is the temple for Satan, and the human psyche became the incarnation of two spirits – either the spirit of El (male) or the spirit of Isis (female) and the spirit of Michael. When the human being embraces the human conscious, she or he embraces the Isis or El spirits located within the left brain and disconnects from the Michael spirit in the subconscious.

Man shall acquire his rightful status on earth's fifth dimension when he stops embracing the false ideologies which was imposed upon his Michael spirit by an Agenda. When he can end his greed of money and when he can curtail his sexual perversions to perceive the human being not through the outward beauty of the physical body but through the inner beauty of the metaphysical spirit, man will be well on his way.

He will accept the inevitable reality: he possesses two spirits, two forces that are vehemently opposed to each other. Those two forces, the conscious and the subconscious, the id and the ego, the ying and the yang, Satan and God, have to be acknowledged and reckoned with if man is to ever transcend himself into his spiritual destiny. One of them, the conscious, controls the13th dimensional mind within the physical world; the other, the subconscious, controls the fifth dimensional mind within the 13th dimensional world.

Man will obtain true knowledge when he discovers his hidden identity through his Michael spirit in the subconscious. Knowledge that is free from the confines of the conscious mind will be everlasting to die not with physical death but to live within the Michael spirit forever, yet knowledge which is obtained through the physical senses of the conscious mind remains superficial, and it like the other earthly desires -- sex, power, wealth, greed – will remain meaningless to man's spiritual evolution and will die along with his conscious mind upon his physical demise.

Once man makes contact with the subconscious he will realize that he possesses two identities; one is living within the conscious mind; the other, within the subconscious. Through his hidden identity -- the subconscious -- man's Michael spirit (his human conscious) will become aware of the subconscious (his unconscious mind), and once this connection occurs, the conscious mind will begun to accept subliminal messages from the subconscious, and man's Michael spirit will consciously choose the right path toward earth's fifth dimension.

Traditional hypnosis, as used for therapeutic purposes, means the hypnotist communicates with the subject's subconscious, but the subject remains unaware of the experience. This means, the hypnotist's human conscious communicates with the subject's subconscious while the subject's human conscious doesn't. On the other hand, self-hypnosis, as accomplished through the simple methods described in chapter two of the book Self-Hypnotism, allows for the subject's entrapped Michael spirit (his human conscious) to communicate directly with the subconscious. This allows the entrapped Michael spirit to communicate directly with the previously disconnected subconscious.

Unknown becomes the fact, self-hypnosis allows man's Michael spirit to re-acquaint and to form a bond with the subconscious. This bond creates a path to the right brain that through repeated incarnations will return the entrapped Michael spirit to the subconscious upon the conscious minds physical death. Since the Age of Pisces, upon the conscious mind's physical demise, the entrapped human spirit is returning to Limbo. Science has yet to re-define the deceitful name of the subconscious and to re-name it the infinite consciousness, for there is nothing sub-standard about it. The subconscious stands supreme over the conscious mind

Thus, man lives unaware of his true identity. Led to believe that he is nothing but flesh and bones, his Michael spirit has fused with his conscious mind. As he lives the conditioned life-style that is created solely to control his human mind, the time will ultimately come when man will lose contact with his subconscious.

Through self-hypnosis, five-percent of the human population could now discover that they received information through the subconscious without being consciously aware. Heavenly messengers have come to earth in their silent-elusive-ever-present lights to plant into five-percent of the human race prophetical knowledge in the hope that someone's conscious mind will finally break free from the confines of human conditioning to discover the information that lies within the recesses of the subconscious.

Hence, it has become the scope and the purpose of this book to unveil to you the reader the opportunity to comprehend and to discover the essence of your true identity. Elohim, Michael, Ra, Viracocha, have stood by man every step of the way, but he refuses to be carried into the light. So he remains alone, cold and isolated. As man embraces the 21st century of consciousness, he will continue to struggle between good and evil. But the day will come when he will shut himself completely from the light, and he will destine himself to follow the path into spiritual darkness to reside within the realm of the fallen angels for an eternity and to wait for another day in consciousness to occur once again on planet earth.

References

Self hypnotism – The Technique and Its Use in Daily Living
Copyright 1964 Leslie M. Lecron
Library of Congress Catalog Number 64-10742
Published by the New American Library, Inc. 1301 Avenue of the Americas, New York, New York 10019

The Interrupted Journey
1966 John G. Fuller
Library of Congress Catalog Number 66-27393
Dial Press New York

The Babylonian Genesis
Second edition 1951
Alexander Heidel
LCN: 51-822
ISBN 0-226-32399-4
The University of Chicago Press 60637
Printed in the United States of America

Forbidden Mysteries of Enoch
Elizabeth Clare Prophet
ISBN 0-916766-60-8
Library of Congress Catalog Card Number: 82-062445
Summit University Press'

Popol Vuh
Copyright 1985 by Dennis Tedlock
First Touchtone Edition 1986
Published by Simon & Schuster
Rockefeller Center
1230 Avenue of the Americas

New York, New York 10020

Roswell Incident
Copyright 1980 Charles Berlitz &William L. Moore
ISBN 0-448-21199-8
Library of Congress Catalog Card Number 80-67075
Grosset & Dunlap Publisher, N.Y.

When Time Began
Zecharia Sitchin
Avon Books

The Twelve Planet
Zecharia Sitcin

Genesis Revisited
Zecharia Sitchin

The Holy Bible
King James Version

http://www.webexhibits.org/calendars/calendar-mayan.html

http://www.ufocasebook.com/walton.html

http://www.huffingtonpost.com/2011/04/30/saif-al-arab-gaddafi-libya-killed_n_855920.html

www.huffingtonpost.com/2011/egypt.revolution

http://newsflavor.com/world/middle.east

http://n.wikipedia.org/wiki/tunisiarevolution

http://abcnews.go.com

http://www.essortment.com/allfamousearthquak_tuwj..html

http://en.wikipedia.org/wiki/Jonestown

http://www.mayan-calendar.com/ancient_long_count.html

http://en.wikipedia.org/wiki/Template:earthquakes_in_2010

http://www.latimes.com/articles/101313

http://metaresearch.org/solar%20system/cydonia/proof_files/proof.asp

http://nssdc.gsfc.nasa.gov/planetary/viking.html